THE QUICK REFERENCE
WORLD ATLAS

SUNBURST BOOKS

Published 1995 by Sunburst Books, Deacon House, 65 Old Church Street, London, SW3 5BS

© European Map Graphics Ltd

Computer Cartography designed and produced by European Map Graphics Ltd.
Alberto House, Hogwood Lane,
Finchampstead, Berkshire.

ISBN 1 85778 165 1

Flags produced by E.M.G. Ltd and authenticated by The Flag Research Center, Winchester, Mass. 01890 U.S.

All rights reserved. No part of this publication may be reproduced, stored in a retrieval system or transmitted in any form or by any means, electronic, mechanical, photocopying, recording or otherwise, without the written permission of the publishers and copyright holder.

Printed and bound in China

Contents

WORLD

World - Key Map	4-5
World - Physical	6-7
World - Ocean Currents	8
World - Earthquake Zones	8
World - Global Warming	9
World - Acid Rain	9
Flags of the Worlds Nations	10-13

EUROPE

Europe - Political	14-15
Albania, Andorra, Austria	16
Belgium, Belarus, Balearic Islands	17
Bosnia Herzegovina, Bulgaria, Croatia	18
Cyprus, Czech Republic, Denmark	19
Estonia, France, Monaco	20
Finland, Germany	21
Greece, Hungary, Iceland	22
Ireland, Italy, San Marino, Vatican City	23
Latvia, Liechtenstein, Lithuania, Luxembourg	24
Macedonia, Malta, Moldova	25
Netherlands, Norway, Poland	26
Portugal, Romania, Slovak Republic	27
Slovenia, Spain, Sweden	28
Switzerland, Turkey, Ukraine, Yugoslavia	29
United Kingdom	30-31

NORTH AND CENTRAL AMERICA

North &Central America -Political	32-33
Antigua & Barbuda, Bahamas, Barbados	34
Belize, Bermuda, Costa Rica	35
Canada, Cuba, Dominica	36
Dominican Republic, El Salvador, Greenland	37
Grenada, Guatemala, Haiti, Honduras	38
Jamaica, Mexico, Nicaragua, Panama	39
Puerto Rico, St. Christopher Nevis, St Lucia, St Vincent	40
Trinidad & Tobago, United States	41

SOUTH AMERICA

South America - Political	42-43
Argentina, Bolivia, Brazil	44
Chile, Colombia, Ecuador	45
Guyana, Paraguay, Peru	46
Surinam, Uruguay, Venezuela	47

AFRICA

Africa - Political	48-49
Algeria, Angola, Azores	50
Benin, Botswana, Burkina Faso	51
Burundi, Cameroon, Canary Islands	52
Cape Verde, Central African Republic, Chad	53
Comoros, Congo, Cote d'Ivoire, Djibouti	54
Egypt, Eritrea, Ethiopia, Equatorial Guinea	55
Gabon, Gambia, Ghana	56
Guinea, Guinea Bissau, Kenya	57
Lesotho, Liberia, Libya	58
Madagascar, Madeira, Malawi	59
Mali, Mauritania, Mauritius	60
Morocco, Mozambique, Namibia	61
Niger, Nigeria, Rwanda	62
São Tomé & Príncipe, Senegal, Seychelles, Sierra Leone	63
Somalia, South Africa, Sudan	64
Swaziland, Tanzania, Togo	65
Tunisia, Uganda, Zaire	66
Zambia, Zimbabwe	67

ASIA

Asia - Political	68-69
Afghanistan, Armenia, Azerbaijan	70
Bahrain, Bangladesh, Bhutan	71
Brunei, Cambodia, Georgia	72
China, Hong Kong	73
India, Indonesia, Iran	74
Iraq, Israel, Japan	75
Jordan, North Korea, South Korea	76
Kazakhstan, Kuwait, Kyrgyzstan	77
Laos, Lebanon, Malaysia	78
Maldives, Mongolia, Myanmar(Burma)	79
Nepal, Oman, Pakistan	80
Philippines, Qatar	81
Russia, Saudi Arabia	82
Singapore, Sri Lanka, Syria	83
Taiwan, Tajikistan, Thailand, Turkmenistan	84
United Arab Emirates, Uzbekistan, Vietnam, Yemen	85

OCEANIA AND POLAR REGIONS

Oceania - Political	86-87
Australia, Fiji, Kiribati & Tuvalu	88
New Zealand, Northern Marianas, Nauru, Marshall Islands	89
Papua New Guinea, Palau, Soloman Islands	90
Tonga, Vanuatu, Western Samoa	91
Arctic & Antarctica	92

Index to Placenames	93-96

Political Key Map

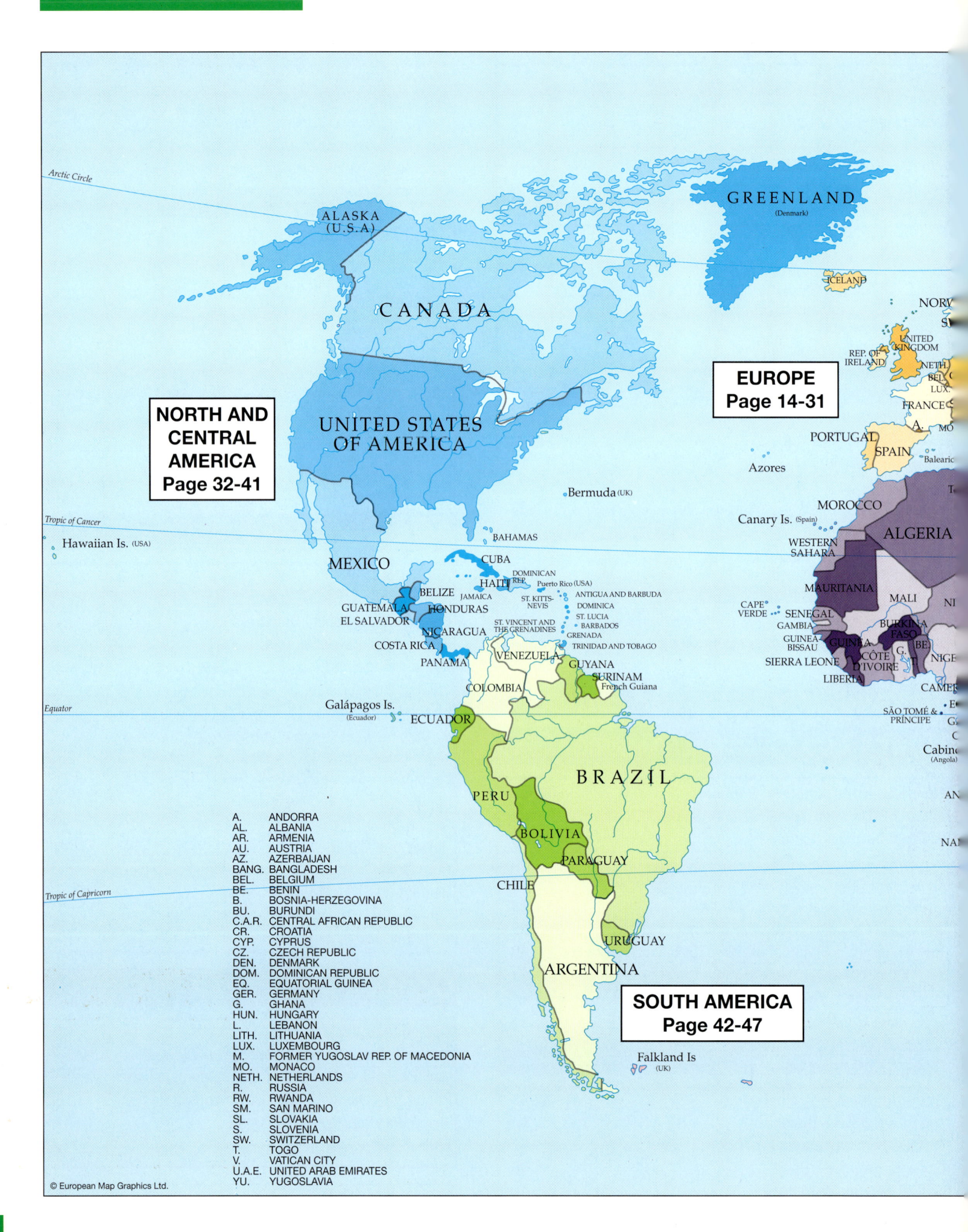

NORTH AND CENTRAL AMERICA
Page 32-41

EUROPE
Page 14-31

SOUTH AMERICA
Page 42-47

A.	ANDORRA
AL.	ALBANIA
AR.	ARMENIA
AU.	AUSTRIA
AZ.	AZERBAIJAN
BANG.	BANGLADESH
BEL.	BELGIUM
BE.	BENIN
B.	BOSNIA-HERZEGOVINA
BU.	BURUNDI
C.A.R.	CENTRAL AFRICAN REPUBLIC
CR.	CROATIA
CYP.	CYPRUS
CZ.	CZECH REPUBLIC
DEN.	DENMARK
DOM.	DOMINICAN REPUBLIC
EQ.	EQUATORIAL GUINEA
GER.	GERMANY
G.	GHANA
HUN.	HUNGARY
L.	LEBANON
LITH.	LITHUANIA
LUX.	LUXEMBOURG
M.	FORMER YUGOSLAV REP. OF MACEDONIA
MO.	MONACO
NETH.	NETHERLANDS
R.	RUSSIA
RW.	RWANDA
SM.	SAN MARINO
SL.	SLOVAKIA
S.	SLOVENIA
SW.	SWITZERLAND
T.	TOGO
V.	VATICAN CITY
U.A.E.	UNITED ARAB EMIRATES
YU.	YUGOSLAVIA

© European Map Graphics Ltd.

POLITICAL KEY MAP

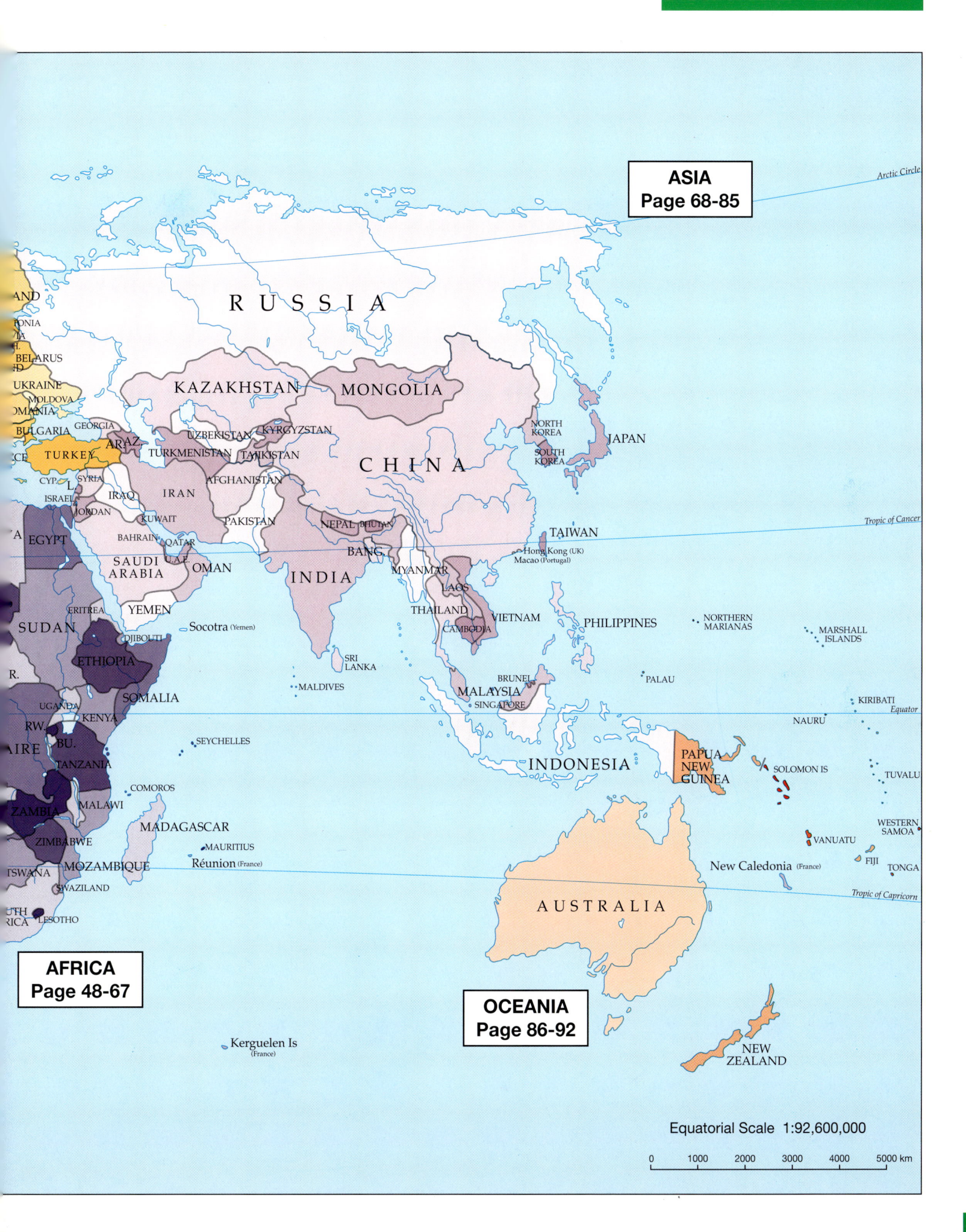

ASIA Page 68-85

AFRICA Page 48-67

OCEANIA Page 86-92

Equatorial Scale 1:92,600,000

0 1000 2000 3000 4000 5000 km

5

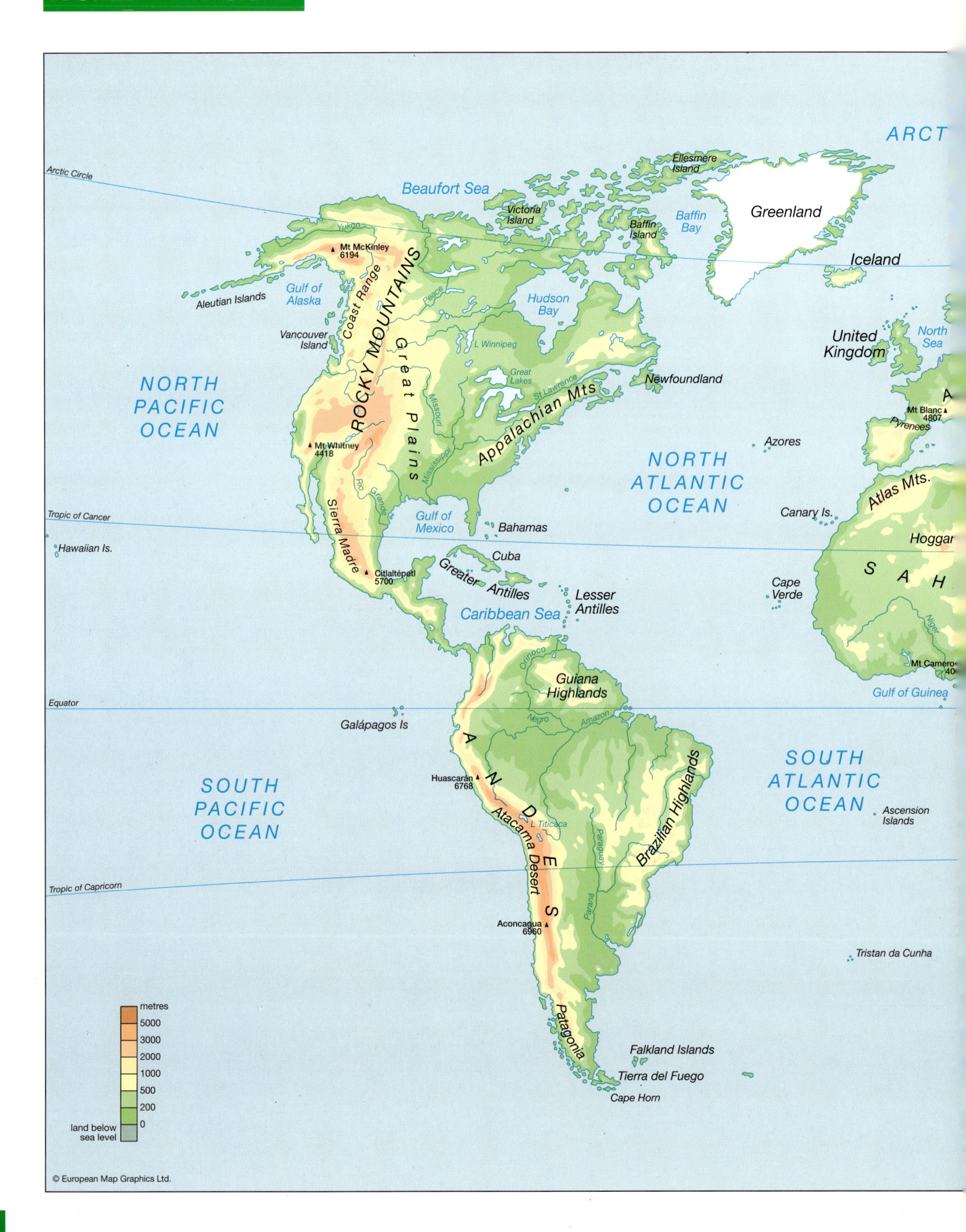

WORLD - PHYSICAL

WORLD - PHYSICAL

Equatorial Scale 1:92,600,000

0 1000 2000 3000 4000 5000 km

Ocean Currents

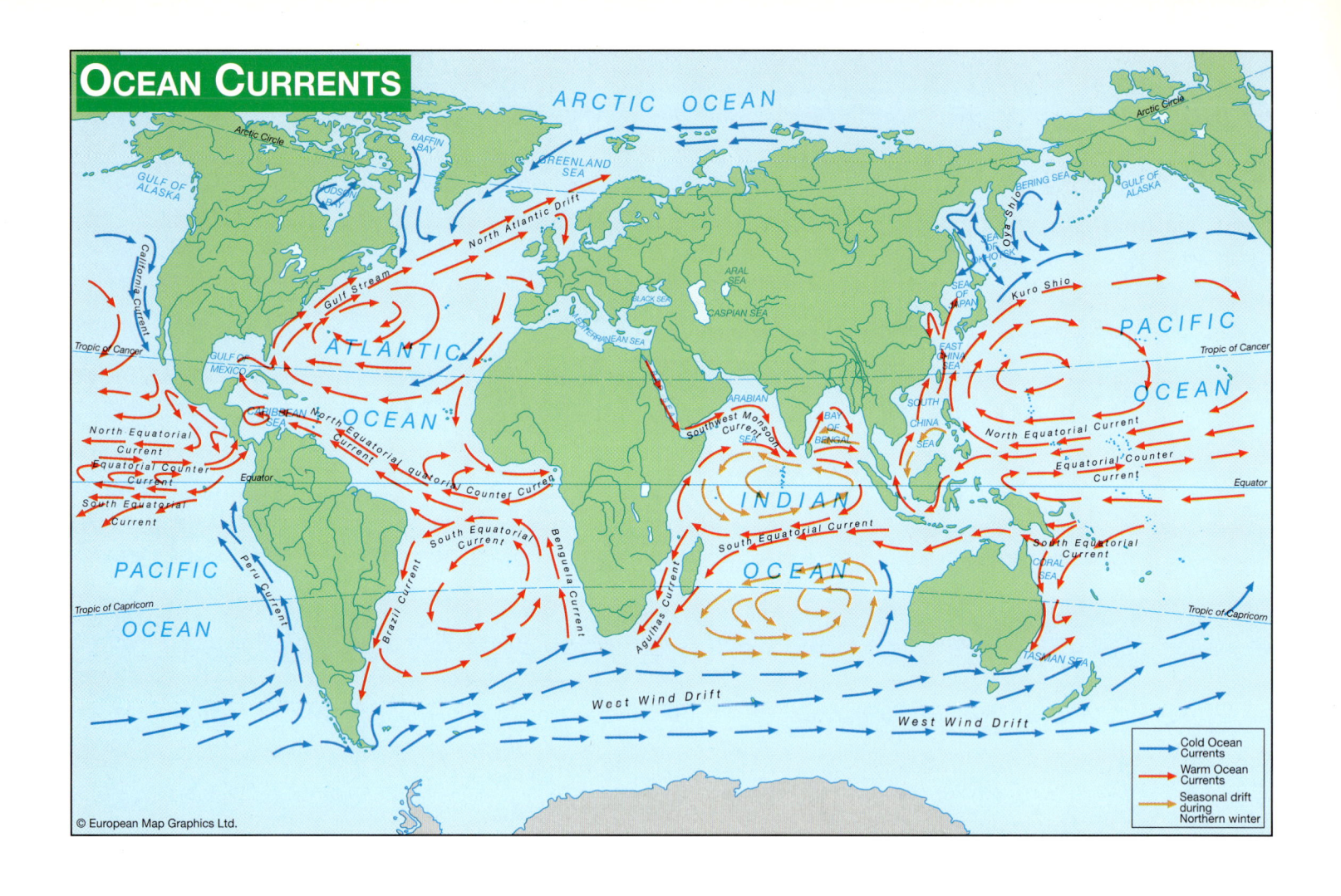

- Cold Ocean Currents
- Warm Ocean Currents
- Seasonal drift during Northern winter

Earthquake Zones

Earth's structural regions
- earthquake zone
- volcano
- transform fault

plate boundaries
- constructive
- destructive
- uncertain

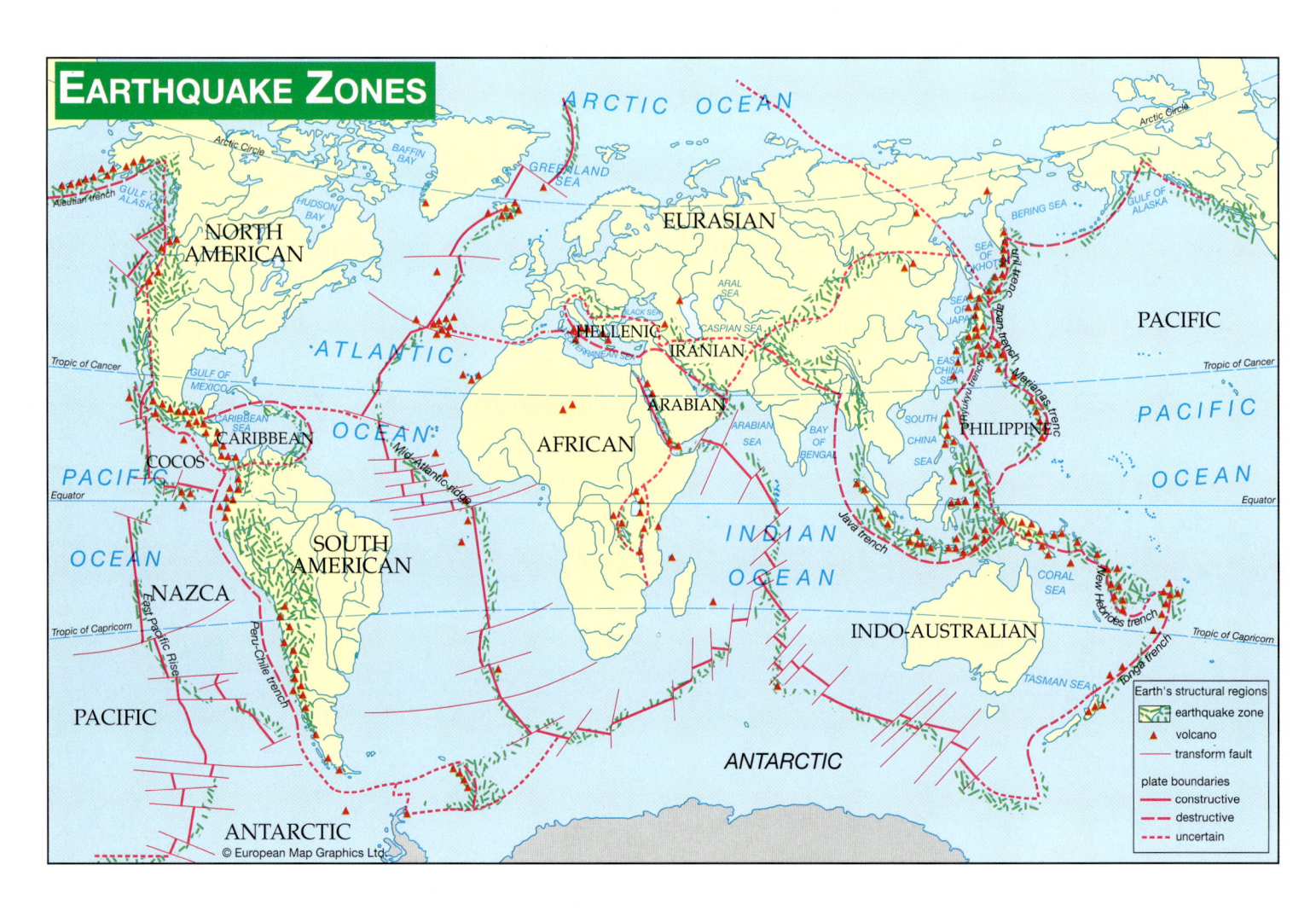

Global Warming

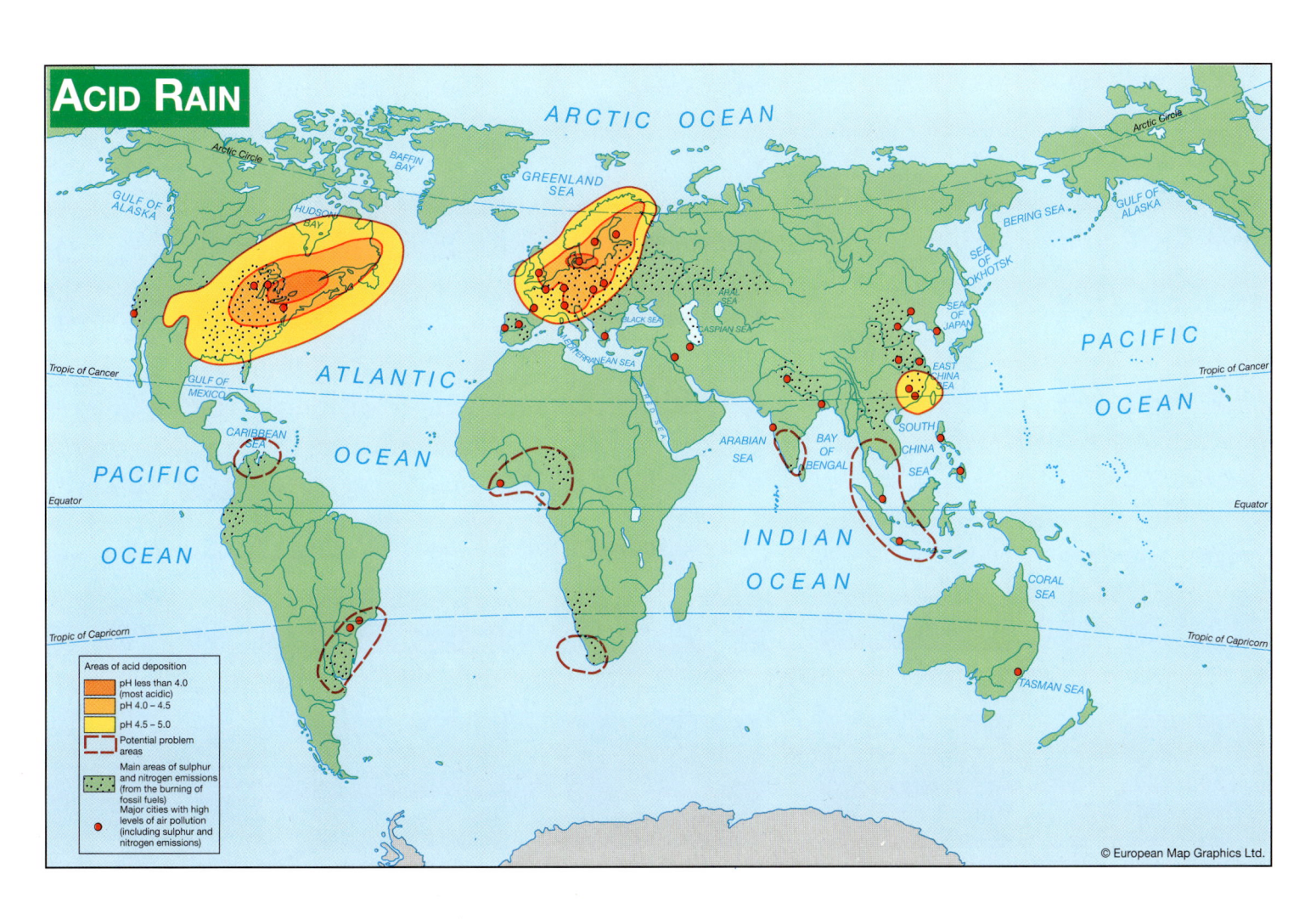

Carbon dioxide (CO₂) emissions in tonnes per person per year
- Over 10 tonnes
- 5 – 10 tonnes
- 1 – 5 tonnes
- Under 1 tonne

Coastal areas vulnerable to rising sea levels caused by global warming

© European Map Graphics Ltd.

Acid Rain

Areas of acid deposition
- pH less than 4.0 (most acidic)
- pH 4.0 – 4.5
- pH 4.5 – 5.0
- Potential problem areas
- Main areas of sulphur and nitrogen emissions (from the burning of fossil fuels)
- Major cities with high levels of air pollution (including sulphur and nitrogen emissions)

© European Map Graphics Ltd.

9

Afghanistan	Azerbaijan	Bhutan	Cameroon	Congo
Albania	Bahamas	Bolivia	Canada	Costa Rica
Algeria	Bahrain	Bosnia-Herzegovina	Cape Verde	Côte d'Ivoire
Andorra	Bangladesh	Botswana	Central African Republic	Croatia
Angola	Barbados	Brazil	Chad	Cuba
Antigua & Barbuda	Belarus	Brunei	Chile	Cyprus
Argentina	Belgium	Bulgaria	China	Czech Republic
Armenia	Belize	Burkina Faso	Colombia	Denmark
Australia	Benin	Burundi	Comoros	Djibouti
Austria		Cambodia		Dominica

Dominican Republic	France	Guinea	Iraq	Kiribati
Ecuador	Gabon	Guinea Bissau	Ireland	Korea, North
Egypt	Gambia	Guyana	Israel	Korea, South
El Salvador	Georgia	Haiti	Italy	Kuwait
Equatorial Guinea	Germany	Honduras	Jamaica	Kyrgyzstan
Eritrea	Ghana	Hungary	Japan	Laos
Estonia	Greece	Iceland	Jordan	Latvia
Ethiopia	Grenada	India	Kazakhstan	Lebanon
Fiji	Guatemala	Indonesia	Kenya	Lesotho
Finland		Iran		Liberia

11

Libya	Malta	Myanmar (Burma)	Northern Marianas	Poland
Liechtenstein	Marshall Islands	Namibia	Norway	Portugal
Lithuania	Mauritania	Nauru	Oman	Qatar
Luxembourg	Mauritius	Nepal	Pakistan	Romania
Macedonia (former Yugoslav republic)	Mexico	Netherlands	Palau	Russia
Madagascar	Moldova	New Zealand	Panama	Rwanda
Malawi	Monaco		Papua New Guinea	St Christopher - Nevis
Malaysia	Mongolia	Nicaragua	Paraguay	Saint Lucia
Maldives	Morocco	Niger	Peru	St Vincent & the Grenadines
Mali	Mozambique	Nigeria	Philippines	San Marino

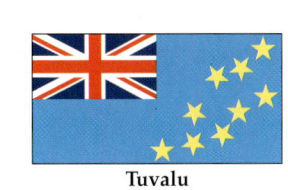

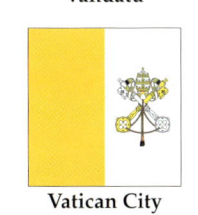

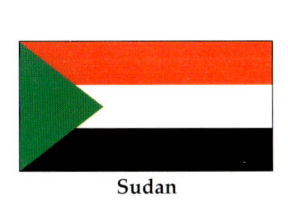

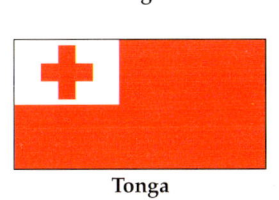

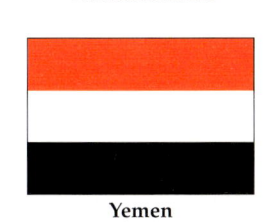

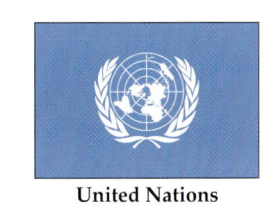

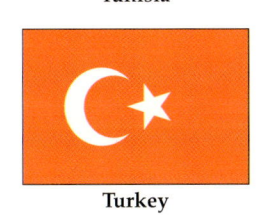

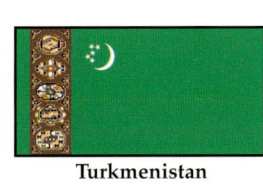

São Tomé & Príncipe	South Africa	Taiwan	Tuvalu	Vanuatu
Saudi Arabia	Spain	Tajikistan	Uganda	Vatican City
Senegal	Sri Lanka	Tanzania	Ukraine	Venezuela
Seychelles	Sudan	Thailand	United Arab Emirates	Vietnam
Sierra Leone	Surinam	Togo	United Kingdom	Western Samoa
Singapore	Swaziland	Tonga	United Nations	Yemen
Slovakia	Sweden	Trinidad & Tobago	United States of America	Yugoslavia
Slovenia	Switzerland	Tunisia	Uruguay	Zaïre
Solomon Islands	Syria	Turkey	Uzbekistan	Zambia
Somalia		Turkmenistan		Zimbabwe

13

EUROPE

EUROPE

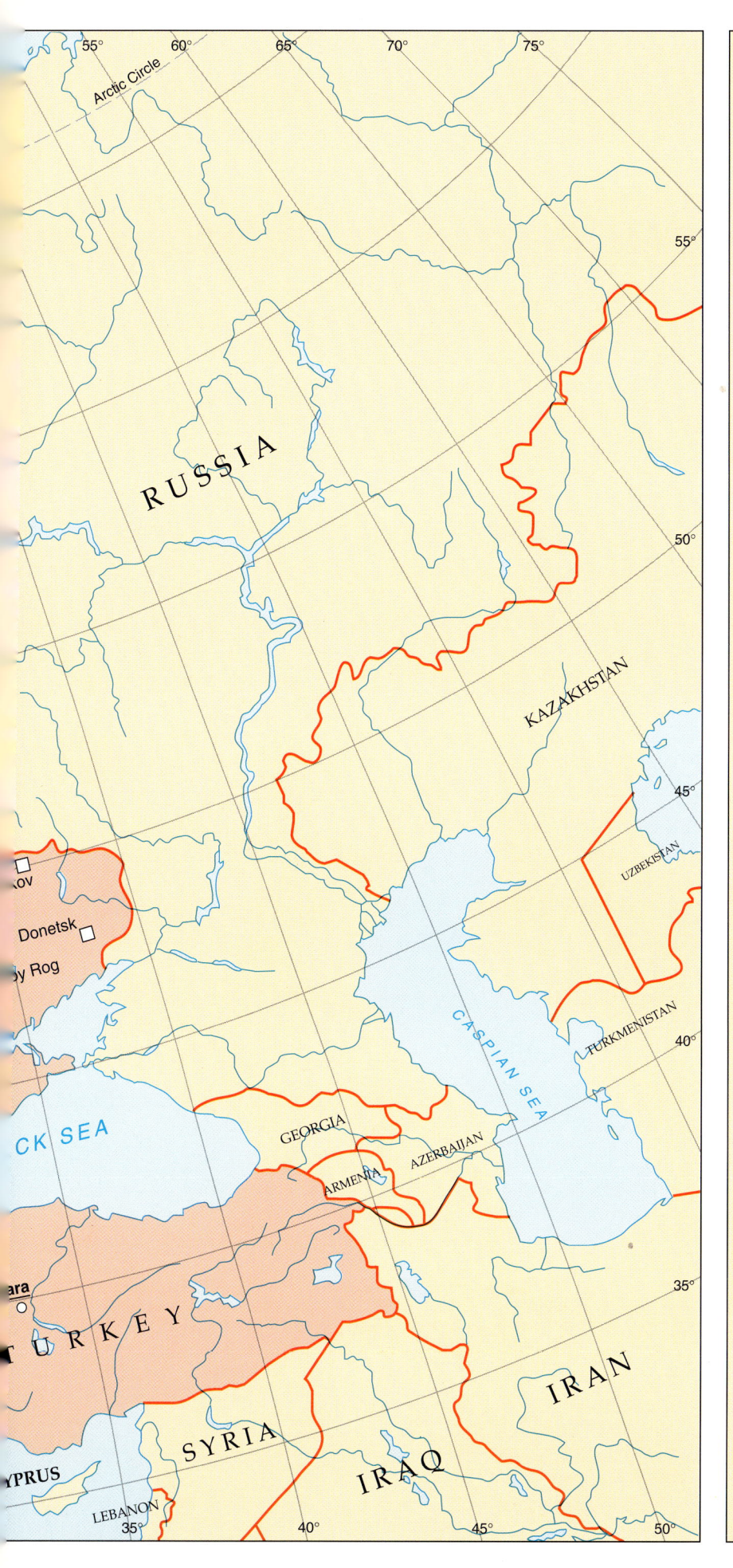

COUNTRY	PAGE
Albania	16
Andorra	16
Austria	16
Balearic Islands	17
Belarus	17
Belgium	17
Bosnia-Herzegovina	18
Bulgaria	18
Croatia	18
Cyprus	19
Czech Republic	19
Denmark	19
England	30
Estonia	20
Finland	21
France	20
Germany	21
Greece	22
Hungary	22
Iceland	22
Ireland	23
Italy	23
Latvia	24
Liechtenstein	24
Lithuania	24
Luxembourg	24
Macedonia (Former Yugoslav Republic)	25
Malta	25
Moldova	25
Monaco	20
Netherlands	26
Northern Ireland	31
Norway	26
Poland	26
Portugal	27
Romania	27
San Marino	23
Scotland	31
Slovakia	27
Slovenia	28
Spain	28
Sweden	28
Switzerland	29
Turkey	29
Ukraine	29
United Kingdom	30
Vatican City	23
Wales	31
Yugoslavia	29

15

ALBANIA

Facts and Figures

Capital: Tiranë 251,000 (1990)
Area (sq km): 28,748
Population: 3,300,000 (1991)
Language: Albanian, Greek, English
Religion: Sunni Muslim 70%
　　　　　Orthodox 20%
　　　　　Roman Catholic 10%
Currency: Lek = 100 quindars
Annual Income per person: $1,000
Annual Trade per person: $73
Adult Literacy: 85%
Life Expectancy (F): 75
Life Expectancy (M): 70

ANDORRA

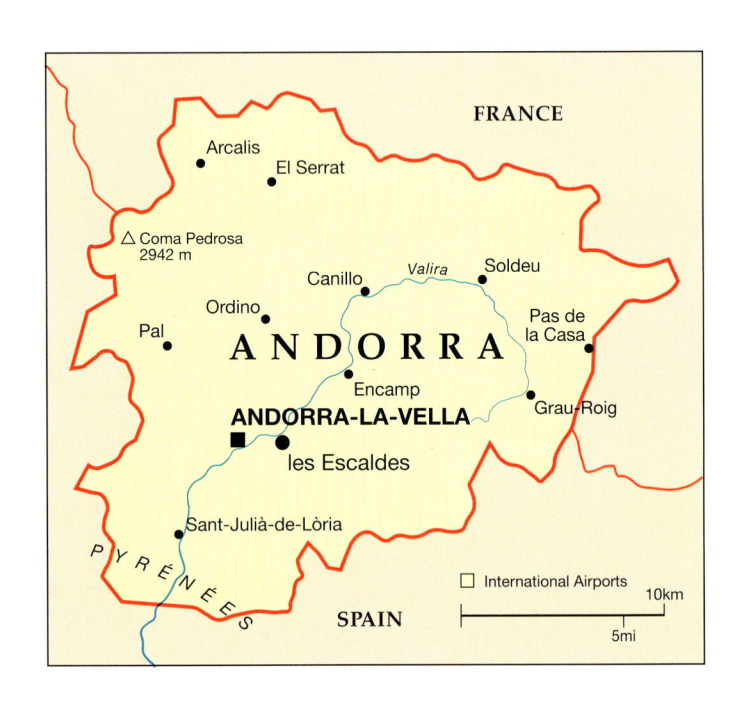

AUSTRIA

Facts and Figures

Capital: Vienna 1,539,850 (1991)
Area (sq km): 83,860
Population: 7,800,000 (1991)
Language: German
Religion: Roman Catholic 78%
　　　　　Protestant 5%
Currency: Schilling = 100 groschen
Annual Income per person: $20,380
Annual Trade per person: $11,653
Adult Literacy: 99%
Life Expectancy (F): 79
Life Expectancy (M): 72

Facts and Figures

Capital: Andorra la vella 19,000 (1990)
Area (sq km): 453
Population: 59,000 (1993)
Language: Catalan, Spanish, French
Religion: Roman Catholic
Currency: French Franc, Spanish Peseta
Annual Income per person: $14,000
Annual Trade per person: $9,000
Adult Literacy: Data not available
Life Expectancy (F): 81
Life Expectancy (M): 74

16

BALEARIC ISLANDS

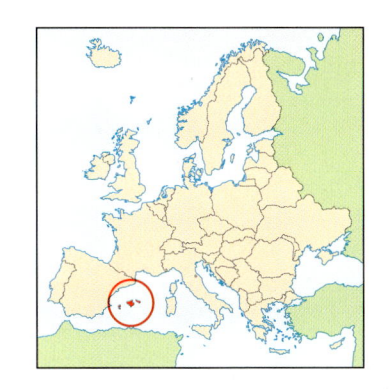

Facts and Figures

Facts and Figures for the Balearic Islands are incorporated within the details given for Spain

BELARUS

Facts and Figures

Capital: Minsk 1,613,000 (1990)
Area (sq km): 207,600
Population: 10,280,000 (1992)
Language: Belorussian, Russian
Religion: Christian Orthodox, Roman Catholic
Currency: Rouble
Annual Income per person: $3,110
Annual Trade per person: $1,000
Adult Literacy: 95%
Life Expectancy (F): 75
Life Expectancy (M): 64

BELGIUM

Facts and Figures

Capital: Brussels 1,331,000 (1991)
Area (sq km): 30,530
Population: 10,020,000 (1992)
Language: Flemish, Dutch, Walloon
Religion: Roman Catholic 72% Protestant
Currency: Belgian Franc
Annual Income per person: $19,300
Annual Trade per person: $23,443
Adult Literacy: 99%
Life Expectancy (F): 79
Life Expectancy (M): 72

BOSNIA-HERZEGOVINA

Facts and Figures

Capital: Sarajevo 526,000 (1991)
Area (sq km): 51,129
Population: 4,366,000 (1991)
Language: Serbo-Croat
Religion: Muslim 40% Orthodox 31%
   Roman Catholic 15%
Currency: Dinar
Annual Income per person: $3,000
Annual Trade per person: $900
Adult Literacy: 86%
Life Expectancy (F): 73
Life Expectancy (M): 68

BULGARIA

Facts and Figures

Capital: Sofia 1,141,140 (1990)
Area (sq km): 110,994
Population: 8,470,000 (1992)
Language: Bulgarian, Turkish, Romany
Religion: Eastern Orthodox 80%
   Sunni Muslim
Currency: Lev = 100 stotinki
Annual Income per person: $1,840
Annual Trade per person: $2,000
Adult Literacy: 93%
Life Expectancy (F): 76
Life Expectancy (M): 70

CROATIA

Facts and Figures

Capital: Zagreb 726,770 (1991)
Area (sq km): 56,540
Population: 4,790,000 (1992)
Language: Serbo-Croat
Religion: Roman Catholic 77%
   Orthodox 11%
Currency: Croatian Dinar
Annual Income per person: $5,600
Annual Trade per person: $1,500
Adult Literacy: 96%
Life Expectancy (F): 74
Life Expectancy (M): 67

CYPRUS

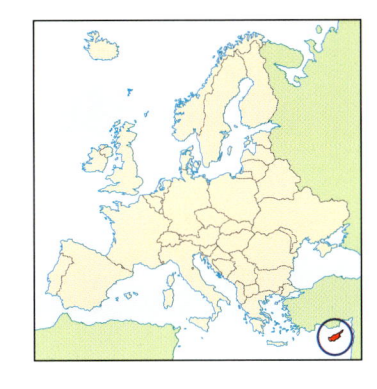

Facts and Figures

Capital: Nicosia 166,500 (1991)
Area (sq km): 9,250
Population: 725,000 (1994)
Language: Greek, Turkish, English
Religion: Greek Orthodox 79%
Muslim 18%
Currency: Cyprus Pound
Annual Income per person: $8,640
Annual Trade per person: $5,032
Adult Literacy: 94%
Life Expectancy (F): 79
Life Expectancy (M): 74

CZECH REPUBLIC

Facts and Figures

Capital: Prague 1,120,000 (1990)
Area (sq km): 79,000
Population: 10,330,000 (1993)
Language: Czech
Religion: Protestant
Currency: Koruna = 100 halura
Annual Income per person: N/A
Annual Trade per person: N/A
Adult Literacy: 99%
Life Expectancy (F): 76
Life Expectancy (M): 69

DENMARK

Facts and Figures

Capital: Copenhagen 1,342,680 (1993)
Area (sq km): 43,075
Population: 5,180,000 (1993)
Language: Danish
Religion: Lutheran 90%
Currency: Krone = 100 øre
Annual Income per person: $23,660
Annual Trade per person: $14,046
Adult Literacy: 99%
Life Expectancy (F): 79
Life Expectancy (M): 73

ESTONIA

Facts and Figures

Capital: Tallinn 502,400 (1991)
Area (sq km): 45,100
Population: 1,600,000 (1992)
Language: Estonian, Russian
Religion: Lutheran, Orthodox
Currency: Kroon = 100 sents
Annual Income per person: $3,830
Annual Trade per person: $850
Adult Literacy: N/A
Life Expectancy (F): 75
Life Expectancy (M): 66

FRANCE

Facts and Figures

Capital: Paris 9,318,800 (1990)
Area (sq km): 543,965
Population: 57,800,000 (1994)
Language: French
Religion: Roman Catholic 73%
Other Christian 4% Muslim 3%
Currency: Franc = 100 centimes
Annual Income per person: $20,600
Annual Trade per person: $8,195
Adult Literacy: 99%
Life Expectancy (F): 81
Life Expectancy (M): 73

MONACO

Facts and Figures

Capital: Monaco
Area (sq km): 1.5
Population: 30,000
Language: French, Monégasque
Religion: Roman Catholic 95%
Currency: French currency
Annual Income per person: $16,000
Annual Trade per person: N/A
Adult Literacy: N/A
Life Expectancy (F): 80
Life Expectancy (M): 72

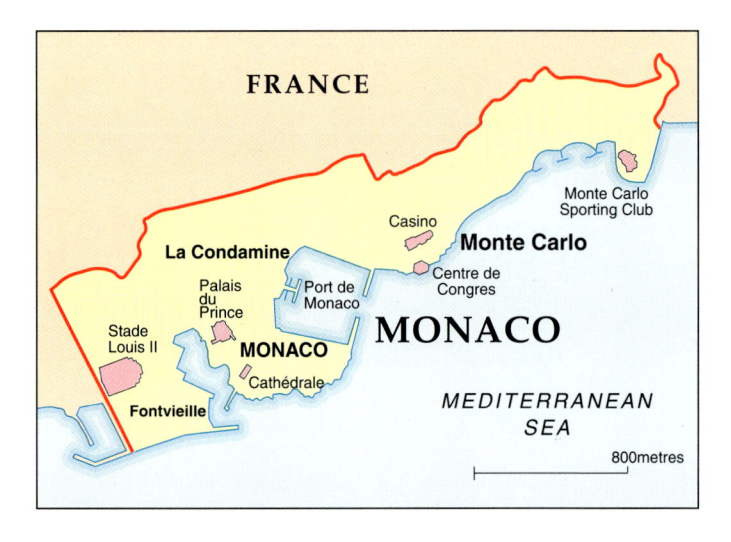

FINLAND

Facts and Figures

Capital: Helsinki 501,500 (1992)
Area (sq km): 338,100
Population: 5,050,000 (1992)
Language: Finnish, Swedish
Religion: Lutheran 87%
Currency: Markka = 100 penniä
Annual Income per person: $21,009
Annual Trade per person: $8,852
Adult Literacy: 99%
Life Expectancy (F): 80
Life Expectancy (M): 72

GERMANY

German Regions

Facts and Figures

Capital: Berlin 3,437,900 (1990)
Area (sq km): 356,700
Population: 80,280,000 (1992)
Language: German
Religion: Protestant 45%
Roman Catholic 35%
Currency: Deutschmark = 100 pfennig
Annual Income per person: $23,650
Annual Trade per person: $12,860
Adult Literacy: 99%
Life Expectancy (F): 78
Life Expectancy (M): 72

GREECE

Facts and Figures

Capital: Athens 3,096,800 (1991)
Area (sq km): 131,960
Population: 10,260,000 (1991)
Language: Greek
Religion: Greek Orthodox 98%
Currency: Drachma = 100 lepta
Annual Income per person: $6,374
Annual Trade per person: $3,005
Adult Literacy: 93%
Life Expectancy (F): 79
Life Expectancy (M): 74

HUNGARY

Facts and Figures

Capital: Budapest 2,016,000 (1992)
Area (sq km): 93,030
Population: 10,310,000 (1993)
Language: Hungarian, Slovak, German
Religion: Roman Catholic 68%
Protestant 25%
Currency: Forint = 100 filler
Annual Income per person: $2,690
Annual Trade per person: $2,109
Adult Literacy: 99%
Life Expectancy (F): 75
Life Expectancy (M): 68

ICELAND

Facts and Figures

Capital: Reykjavik 100,850 (1992)
Area (sq km): 103,000
Population: 262,190 (1992)
Language: Icelandic
Religion: Lutheran 92%
Currency: Króna = 100 aurar
Annual Income per person: $24,570
Annual Trade per person: $12,592
Adult Literacy: 99%
Life Expectancy (F): 81
Life Expectancy (M): 75

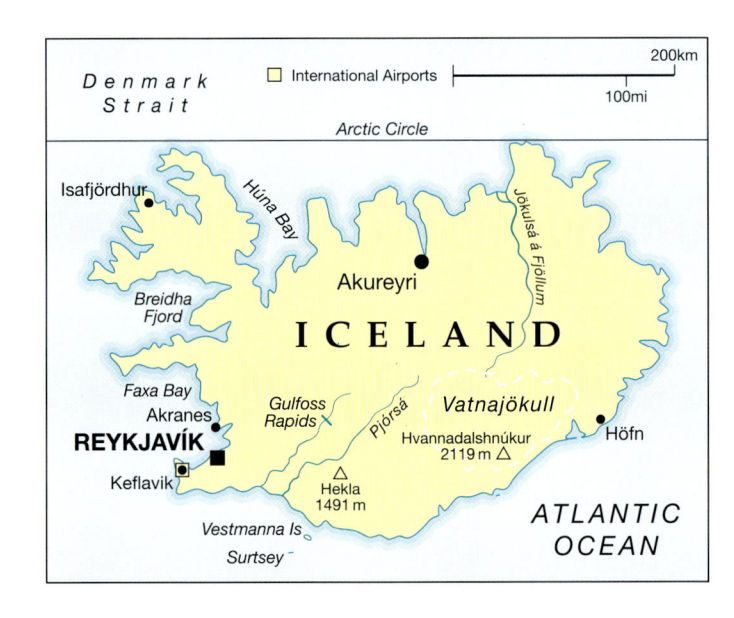

IRELAND

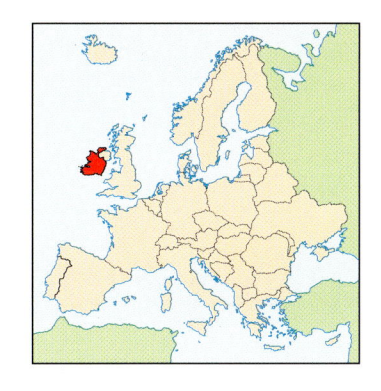

Facts and Figures

Capital: Dublin 915,516 (1991)
Area (sq km): 70,280
Population: 3,550,000 (1992)
Language: Irish, English
Religion: Roman Catholic 90%
Protestant 3%
Currency: Punt = 100 pence
Annual Income per person: $10,780
Annual Trade per person: $14,305
Adult Literacy: 99%
Life Expectancy (F): 78
Life Expectancy (M): 73

ITALY

Vatican City — Facts and Figures

Area (sq km): 0.44
Population: 1,000
Language: Latin, Italian
Religion: Roman Catholic
Currency: Vatican Lira
Annual Income per person: N/A
Annual Trade per person: N/A
Adult Literacy: N/A
Life Expectancy (F): N/A
Life Expectancy (M): N/A

San Marino — Facts and Figures

Capital: San Marino
Area (sq km): 61
Population: 24,000
Language: Italian
Religion: Roman Catholic
Currency: Lira
Annual Income per person: $17,000
Annual Trade per person: N/A
Adult Literacy: 96%
Life Expectancy (F): 79
Life Expectancy (M): 74

Italy — Facts and Figures

Capital: Rome 2,723,330 (1992)
Area (sq km): 301,300
Population: 56,960,000 (1992)
Language: Italian
Religion: Roman Catholic 84%
Currency: Lira
Annual Income per person: $18,580
Annual Trade per person: $6,192
Adult Literacy: 97%
Life Expectancy (F): 80
Life Expectancy (M): 73

LATVIA

Facts and Figures

Capital: Riga 910,200 (1991)
Area (sq km): 63,700
Population: 2,610,000 (1993)
Language: Latvian, Russian
Religion: Lutheran
Currency: Lat = 100 santims
Annual Income per person: $3,410
Annual Trade per person: $3,400
Adult Literacy: Data not available
Life Expectancy (F): 75
Life Expectancy (M): 64

LITHUANIA

Facts and Figures

Capital: Vilnius 592,500 (1990)
Area (sq km): 65,200
Population: 3,740,000 (1994)
Language: Lithuanian, Russian
Religion: Roman Catholic 90%, Lutheran
Currency: Litas = 100 centas
Annual Income per person: $2,710
Annual Trade per person: N/A
Adult Literacy: N/A
Life Expectancy (F): 76
Life Expectancy (M): 66

LIECHTENSTEIN

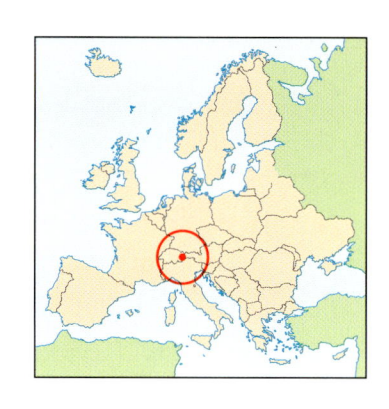

Facts and Figures

Capital: Vaduz
Area (sq km): 157
Population: 30,000
Language: German
Religion: Roman Catholic
Currency: Swiss currency
Annual Income per person: $33,000
Annual Trade per person: N/A
Adult Literacy: 99%
Life Expectancy (F): 81
Life Expectancy (M): 73

LUXEMBOURG

Facts and Figures

Capital: Luxembourg 75,377 (1991)
Area (sq km): 2,590
Population: 395,200 (1993)
Language: Letzeburgish, French, German
Religion: Roman Catholic 95%
Currency: Luxembourg Franc = 100 centimes
Annual Income per person: $31,080
Annual Trade per person: $35,000
Adult Literacy: 100%
Life Expectancy (F): 79
Life Expectancy (M): 72

MACEDONIA

Facts and Figures

Capital: Skopje 448,230 (1991)
Area (sq km): 25,700
Population: 2,060,000 (1992)
Language: Macedonian, Albanian
Religion: Orthodox 67% Muslim 30%
Currency: Dinar = 100 deni
Annual Income per person: $3,100
Annual Trade per person: $800
Adult Literacy: 89%
Life Expectancy (F): 72
Life Expectancy (M): 68

MALTA

Facts and Figures

Capital: Valletta 101,750 (1990)
Area (sq km): 316
Population: 364,600 (1993)
Language: Maltese, English
Religion: Roman Catholic 98%
Currency: Maltese Lira = 100 cents
Annual Income per person: $7,341
Annual Trade per person: $9,311
Adult Literacy: 85%
Life Expectancy (F): 76
Life Expectancy (M): 72

MOLDOVA

Facts and Figures

Capital: Chisinau 676,000 (1990)
Area (sq km): 33,700
Population: 4,400,000 (1992)
Language: Moldavian, Russian
Religion: Russian Orthodox, Evangelical
Currency: Leu
Annual Income per person: $2,170
Annual Trade per person: N/A
Adult Literacy: N/A
Life Expectancy (F): 72
Life Expectancy (M): 65

NETHERLANDS

Facts and Figures

Capital: Amsterdam 719,860 (1993)
Area (sq km): 41,530
Population: 15,240,000 (1993)
Language: Dutch
Religion: Roman Catholic 33%
Protestant 23%
Currency: Guilder = 100 cents
Annual Income per person: $21,030
Annual Trade per person: $18,137
Adult Literacy: 99%
Life Expectancy (F): 81
Life Expectancy (M): 74

NORWAY

Facts and Figures

Capital: Oslo 473,350 (1992)
Area (sq km): 323,880
Population: 4,300,000 (1992)
Language: Norwegian, Lappish, Finnish
Religion: Lutheran 88% Roman Catholic
Currency: Norwegian Krone = 100 øre
Annual Income per person: $24,160
Annual Trade per person: $14,125
Adult Literacy: 99%
Life Expectancy (F): 81
Life Expectancy (M): 74

POLAND

Facts and Figures

Capital: Warsaw 1,655,000 (1989)
Area (sq km): 312,680
Population: 38,310,000 (1993)
Language: Polish
Religion: Roman Catholic 94%
Currency: Zloty = 100 groszy
Annual Income per person: $1,830
Annual Trade per person: $751
Adult Literacy: 99%
Life Expectancy (F): 76
Life Expectancy (M): 67

PORTUGAL

Facts and Figures

Capital: Lisbon 830,500 (1987)
Area (sq km): 91,900
Population: 9,860,000 (1991)
Language: Portuguese
Religion: Roman Catholic
Currency: Escudo = 100 centavos
Annual Income per person: $5,620
Annual Trade per person: $4,836
Adult Literacy: 98%
Life Expectancy (F): 78
Life Expectancy (M): 71

ROMANIA

Facts and Figures

Capital: Bucharest 2,351,000 (1992)
Area (sq km): 237,500
Population: 22,760,000 (1992)
Language: Romanian, Hungarian, German
Religion: Romanian Orthodox 87% RC 5%
Currency: Leu = 100 bani
Annual Income per person: $1,340
Annual Trade per person: $680
Adult Literacy: 96%
Life Expectancy (F): 74
Life Expectancy (M): 69

SLOVAK REPUBLIC

Facts and Figures

Capital: Bratislava 440,421 (1990)
Area (sq km): 49,035
Population: 5,334,000 (1992)
Language: Slovak
Religion: Roman Catholic 22%
Currency: Slovak Koruna
Annual Income per person: N/A
Annual Trade per person: N/A
Adult Literacy: 99%
Life Expectancy (F): 76
Life Expectancy (M): 69

SLOVENIA

Facts and Figures

Capital: Ljubljana 268,000 (1991)
Area (sq km): 20,251
Population: 2,000,000 (1992)
Language: Slovene, Serbo-Croat
Religion: Roman Catholic 94%
Currency: Slovene Tolar
Annual Income per person: $10,000
Annual Trade per person: $5,000
Adult Literacy: 99%
Life Expectancy (F): 75
Life Expectancy (M): 67

SPAIN

Facts and Figures

Capital: Madrid 2,909,800 (1991)
Area (sq km): 504,750
Population: 39,080,000 (1992)
Language: Castilian Spanish, Basque, Catalan, Galician
Religion: Roman Catholic 97%
Currency: Peseta
Annual Income per person: $14,290
Annual Trade per person: $3,934
Adult Literacy: 96%
Life Expectancy (F): 80
Life Expectancy (M): 74

SWEDEN

Facts and Figures

Capital: Stockholm 684,580 (1992)
Area (sq km): 449,960
Population: 8,700,000 (1992)
Language: Swedish, Finnish
Religion: Lutheran 89%
Currency: Krona = 100 öre
Annual Income per person: $25,490
Annual Trade per person: $12,158
Adult Literacy: 99%
Life Expectancy (F): 81
Life Expectancy (M): 75

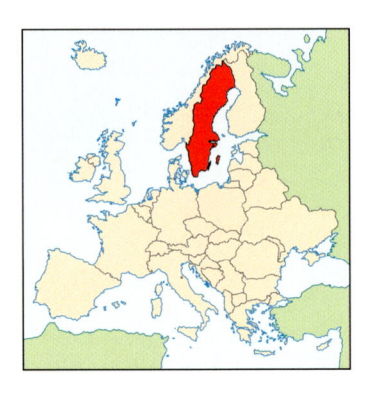

SWITZERLAND

Facts and Figures

Capital: Bern 298,700 (1990)
Area (sq km): 41,130
Population: 6,900,000 (1993)
Language: German, French, Italian, Romansch
Religion: Protestant 47%, Roman Catholic 46%
Currency: Swiss Franc = 100 centimes
Annual Income per person: $32,250
Annual Trade per person: $19,088
Adult Literacy: 99%
Life Expectancy (F): 81
Life Expectancy (M): 75

TURKEY

Facts and Figures

Capital: Ankara 3,022,000 (1990)
Area (sq km): 779,450
Population: 59,870,000 (1993)
Language: Turkish, Kurdish
Religion: Sunni Muslim 64%, Shi'ite Muslim 28%
Currency: Turkish Lira = 100 kurus
Annual Income per person: $1,820
Annual Trade per person: $586
Adult Literacy: 81%
Life Expectancy (F): 68
Life Expectancy (M): 65

UKRAINE

Facts and Figures

Capital: Kiev 2,616,000 (1990)
Area (sq km): 603,700
Population: 52,100,000 (1992)
Language: Ukrainian, Russian
Religion: Ukrainian Orthodox, Roman Catholic
Currency: Rouble = 100 kopeks
Annual Income per person: $2,340
Annual Trade per person: $600
Adult Literacy: Data not available
Life Expectancy (F): 75
Life Expectancy (M): 66

YUGOSLAVIA pre 1991

Facts and Figures

Capital: Belgrade 1,168,000 (1991)
Area (sq km): 102,000
Population: 10,460,000 (1992)
Language: Serbo-Croat
Religion: Orthodox 65%, Muslim 19%
Currency: Dinar = 100 paras
Annual Income per person: $4,500
Annual Trade per person: $1,000
Adult Literacy: 89%
Life Expectancy (F): 75
Life Expectancy (M): 69

UNITED KINGDOM

Facts and Figures

Capital: London 6,679,700 (1991)
Area (sq km): 242,516
Population: 58,000,000
Language: English, Welsh, Scots-Gaelic
Religion: Anglican 57%
Roman Catholic 13%
Currency: Pound Sterling =100 pence
Annual Income per person: $16,080
Annual Trade per person: $7,140
Adult Literacy: 99%
Life Expectancy (F): 79
Life Expectancy (M): 73

ENGLAND

Facts and Figures

Capital: London 6,679,700 (1991)
Area (sq km): 130,439
Population: 47,536,000
Language: English
Religion: Protestant, Roman Catholic, Judaism, Islam
Currency: Pound Sterling = 100 pence
Annual Income per person:
Annual Trade per person:
Adult Literacy:
Life Expectancy (F):
Life Expectancy (M):

English Counties

1. NORTHUMBERLAND
2. TYNE & WEAR
3. DURHAM
4. CLEVELAND
5. CUMBRIA
6. LANCASHIRE
7. MERSEYSIDE
8. GREATER MANCHESTER
9. CHESHIRE
10. NORTH YORKSHIRE
11. WEST YORKSHIRE
12. SOUTH YORKSHIRE
13. HUMBERSIDE
14. LINCOLNSHIRE
15. NOTTINGHAMSHIRE
16. DERBYSHIRE
17. LEICESTERSHIRE
18. NORTHAMPTONSHIRE
19. CAMBRIDGESHIRE
20. NORFOLK
21. SUFFOLK
22. STAFFORDSHIRE
23. SHROPSHIRE
24. WEST MIDLANDS
25. WARWICKSHIRE
26. HEREFORD & WORCESTER
27. OXFORDSHIRE
28. BUCKINGHAMSHIRE
29. BEDFORDSHIRE
30. HERTFORDSHIRE
31. GREATER LONDON
32. ESSEX
33. KENT
34. EAST SUSSEX
35. WEST SUSSEX
36. SURREY
37. BERKSHIRE
38. HAMPSHIRE
39. ISLE OF WIGHT
40. GLOUCESTERSHIRE
41. AVON
42. WILTSHIRE
43. DORSET
44. SOMERSET
45. DEVON
46. CORNWALL & ISLES OF SCILLY

NORTHERN IRELAND

Facts and Figures

Capital: Belfast 300,000
Area (sq km): 14,121
Population: 1,578,000
Language: English
Religion: Protestant, Roman Catholic
Currency: Pound Sterling = 100 pence
Annual Income per person:
Annual Trade per person:
Adult Literacy:
Life Expectancy (F):
Life Expectancy (M):

N. I. Counties

WALES

Facts and Figures

Capital: Cardiff 284,000
Area (sq km): 20,768
Population: 2,857,000
Language: English, Welsh
Religion: Protestant, Roman Catholic
Currency: Pound Sterling = 100 pence
Annual Income per person:
Annual Trade per person:
Adult Literacy:
Life Expectancy (F):
Life Expectancy (M):

Welsh Counties

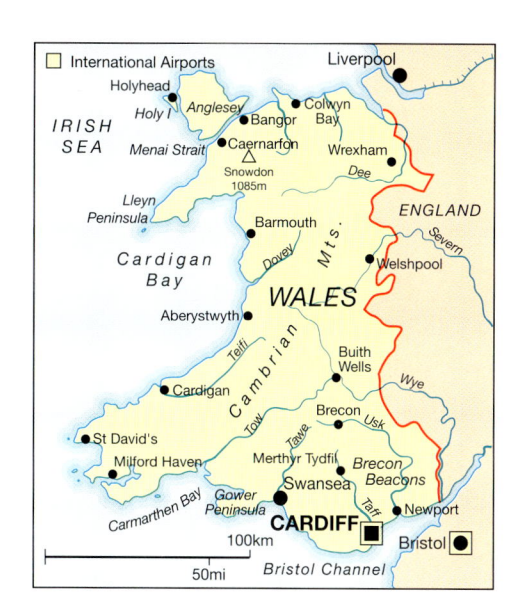

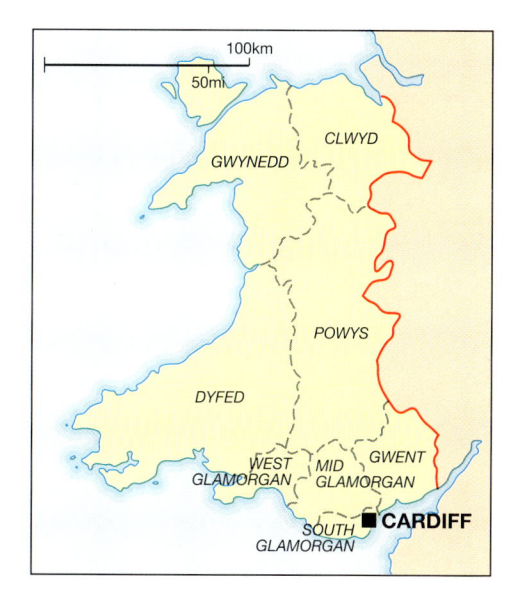

SCOTLAND

Facts and Figures

Capital: Edinburgh 433,000
Area (sq km): 78,772
Population: 5,094,000
Language: English
Religion: Protestant, Roman Catholic
Currency: Pound Sterling = 100 pence
Annual Income per person:
Annual Trade per person:
Adult Literacy:
Life Expectancy (F):
Life Expectancy (M):

Scottish Regions

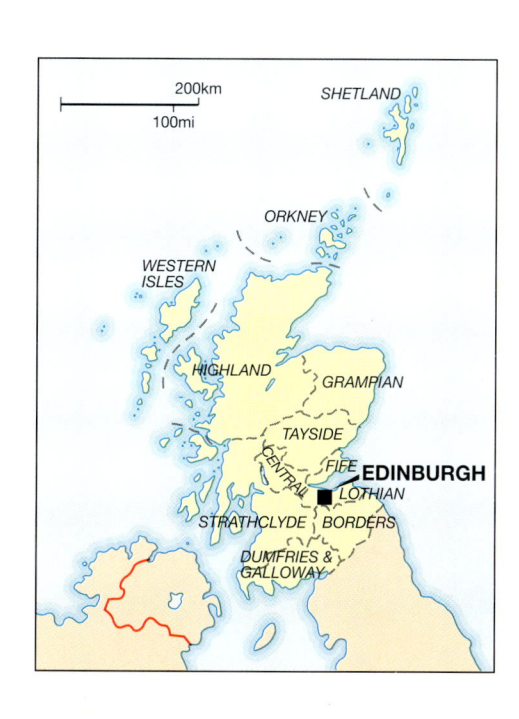

NORTH AND CENTRAL AMERICA

NORTH AND CENTRAL AMERICA

COUNTRY	PAGE
Antigua & Barbuda	34
Bahamas	34
Barbados	34
Bermuda	35
Belize	35
Canada	36
Costa Rica	35
Cuba	36
Dominica	37
Dominican Republic	37
El Salvador	37
Greenland	37
Grenada	38
Guatemala	38
Haiti	38
Honduras	38
Jamaica	39
Mexico	39
Nicaragua	39
Panama	39
Puerto Rico	40
St. Christopher-Nevis	40
St. Lucia	40
St. Vincent and the Grenadines	40
Trinidad & Tobago	41
United States	41

33

ANTIGUA & BARBUDA

Facts and Figures

Capital: St. John's 30,000 (1982)
Area (sq km): 442
Population: 77,000 (1991)
Language: English
Religion: Protestant
Currency: Eastern Caribbean Dollar
Annual Income per person: $4,770
Annual Trade per person: N/A
Adult Literacy: 96%
Life Expectancy (F): 74
Life Expectancy (M): 70

ANTIGUA

- International Airports
- ATLANTIC OCEAN
- St John's Harbour
- VC Bird Int'l Airport
- **ST JOHN'S**
- Five Islands Harbour
- Indian Town Point
- All Saints
- Boggy Peak 405m
- Johnsons Point
- English Harbour Town
- Willoughby Bay
- Redonda

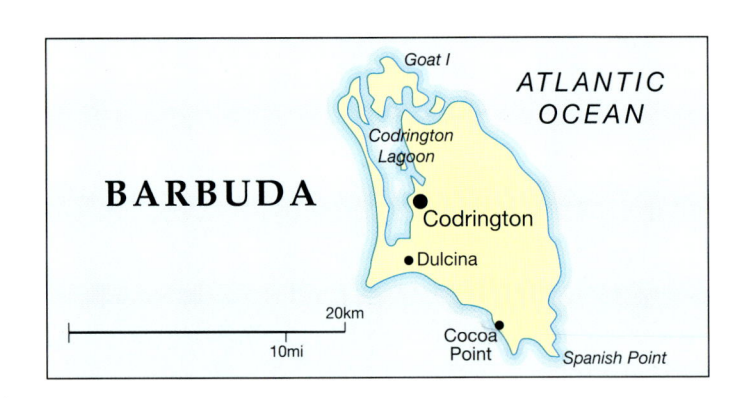

BARBUDA

- Goat I
- ATLANTIC OCEAN
- Codrington Lagoon
- Codrington
- Dulcina
- Cocoa Point
- Spanish Point
- 20km / 10mi

BAHAMAS

BAHAMAS map

- Grand Bahama
- Great Abaco
- Freeport
- Bimini
- Berry Is.
- Eleuthera
- Governor's Harbour
- **NASSAU**
- New Providence I.
- Andros Town
- Andros
- Great Bahama Bank
- ATLANTIC OCEAN
- Cat Island
- San Salvador
- Rum Cay
- Great Exuma
- Tropic of Cancer
- Samana Cay
- Long I.
- Crooked I.
- Acklins I.
- Mayaguana
- Little Inagua
- Great Inagua
- Matthew Town
- CUBA
- 200km / 100mi
- International Airports

Facts and Figures

Capital: Nassau 172,000 (1990)
Area (sq km): 13,864
Population: 264,000 (1992)
Language: English, Creole
Religion: Protestant 69%
 Roman Catholic 26%
Currency: Bahamian Dollar
Annual Income per person: $11,720
Annual Trade per person: $21,531
Adult Literacy: 99%
Life Expectancy (F): 76
Life Expectancy (M): 69

BARBADOS

Facts and Figures

Capital: Bridgetown 6,720 (1990)
Area (sq km): 430
Population: 258,600 (1991)
Language: English, Creole
Religion: Protestant 56%
 Roman Catholic 4%
Currency: Barbados Dollar
Annual Income per person: $6,630
Annual Trade per person: $3,450
Adult Literacy: 99%
Life Expectancy (F): 78
Life Expectancy (M): 73

BARBADOS map

- North Point
- Harrison Point
- Speightstown
- Belleplaine
- Mt Hillaby 340m
- Holetown
- Blackmans
- Constitution
- Ragged Point
- **BRIDGETOWN**
- The Crane
- Worthing
- Hastings
- Grantley Adams Airport
- South Point
- ATLANTIC OCEAN
- 10km / 5mi
- International Airports

BELIZE

Facts and Figures

Capital: Belmopan 5,276 (1990)
Area (sq km): 22,960
Population: 230,000 (1993)
Language: English, Creole, Spanish
Religion: Roman Catholic 62%
　　　　　Protestant 28%
Currency: Belize Dollar
Annual Income per person: $2,050
Annual Trade per person: $1,953
Adult Literacy: 95%
Life Expectancy (F): 72
Life Expectancy (M): 67

BERMUDA

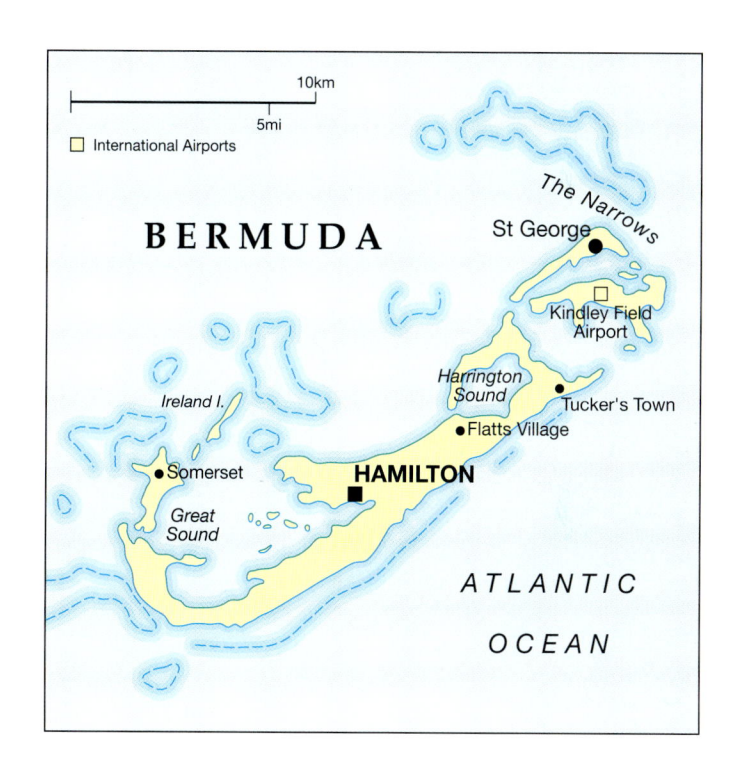

Facts and Figures

Capital: Hamilton 3,440 (1990)
Area (sq km): 53
Population: 71,950 (1992)
Language: English
Religion: Protestant 62%
　　　　　Roman Catholic 14%
Currency: Bermuda Dollar
Annual Income per person: $24,000
Annual Trade per person: $9,750
Adult Literacy: 98%
Life Expectancy (F): 78
Life Expectancy (M): 72

COSTA RICA

Facts and Figures

Capital: San José 245,000 (1984)
Area (sq km): 51,100
Population: 3,300,000 (1991)
Language: Spanish, Creole
Religion: Roman Catholic 90%
Currency: Colon=100 céntimos
Annual Income per person: $1,930
Annual Trade per person: $1,110
Adult Literacy: 93%
Life Expectancy (F): 78
Life Expectancy (M): 73

CANADA

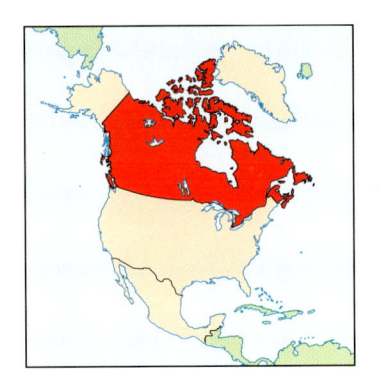

Facts and Figures

Capital: Ottawa 314,000 (1991)
Area (sq km): 9,970,610
Population: 27,400,000 (1992)
Language: English, French
Religion: Roman Catholic 47%
Protestant 41%
Currency: Canadian Dollar
Annual Income per person: $21,260
Annual Trade per person: $9,355
Adult Literacy: 99%
Life Expectancy (F): 81
Life Expectancy (M): 74

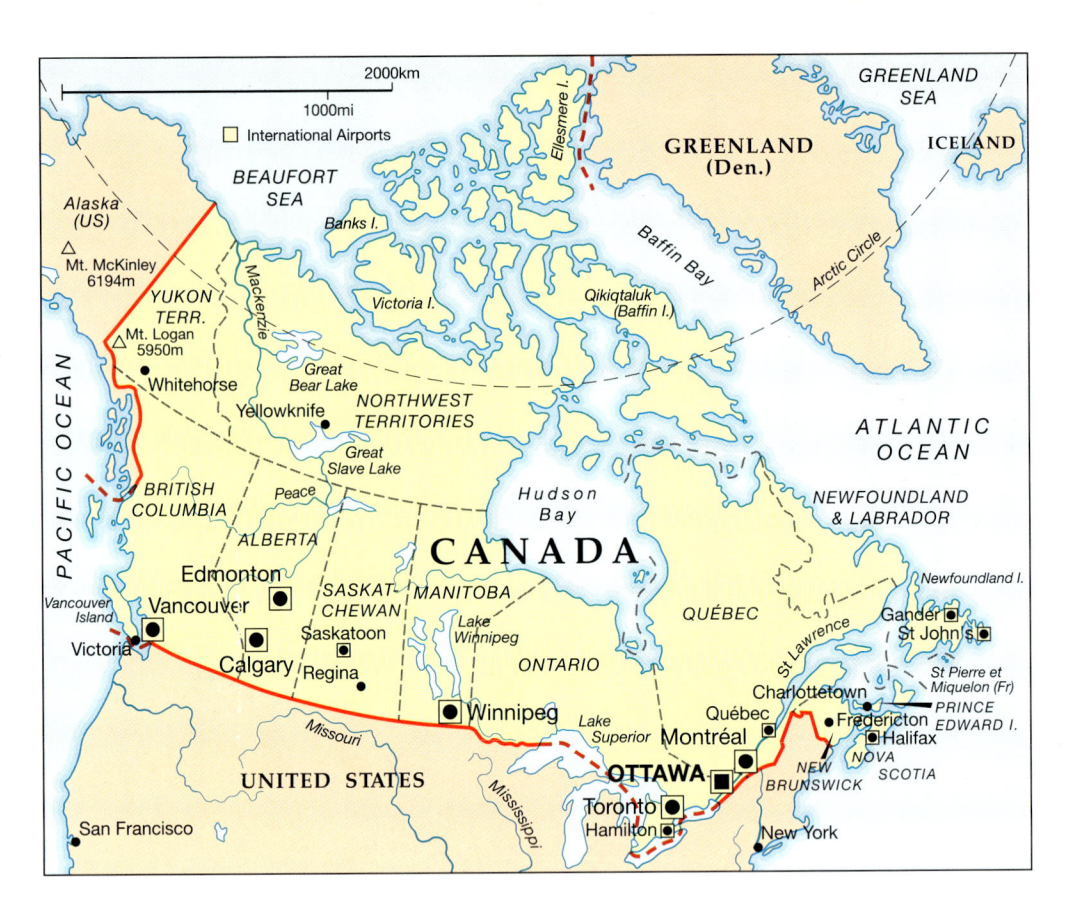

CUBA

Facts and Figures

Capital: Havana 2,014,800 (1986)
Area (sq km): 110,860
Population: 10,700,000 (1991)
Language: Spanish
Religion: Roman Catholic 39%
Protestant 3%
Currency: Cuban peso =100 centavos
Annual Income per person: $1,000
Annual Trade per person: $678
Adult Literacy: 75%
Life Expectancy (F): 78
Life Expectancy (M): 74

DOMINICA

Facts and Figures

Capital: Roseau 20,000 (1991)
Area (sq km): 751
Population: 108,800 (1991)
Language: English, French patois
Religion: Roman Catholic 80%
Protestant 15%
Currency: East Caribbean Dollar
= 100 cents
Annual Income per person: $2,440
Annual Trade per person: $2,163
Adult Literacy: 97%
Life Expectancy (F): 79
Life Expectancy (M): 73

36

DOMINICAN REPUBLIC

Facts and Figures

Capital: Santo Domingo 1,601,000 (1986)
Area (sq km): 48,442
Population: 7,310,000 (1991)
Language: Spanish
Religion: Roman Catholic 92%
Currency: Peso = 100 centavos
Annual Income per person: $950
Annual Trade per person: $324
Adult Literacy: 83%
Life Expectancy (F): 70
Life Expectancy (M): 65

EL SALVADOR

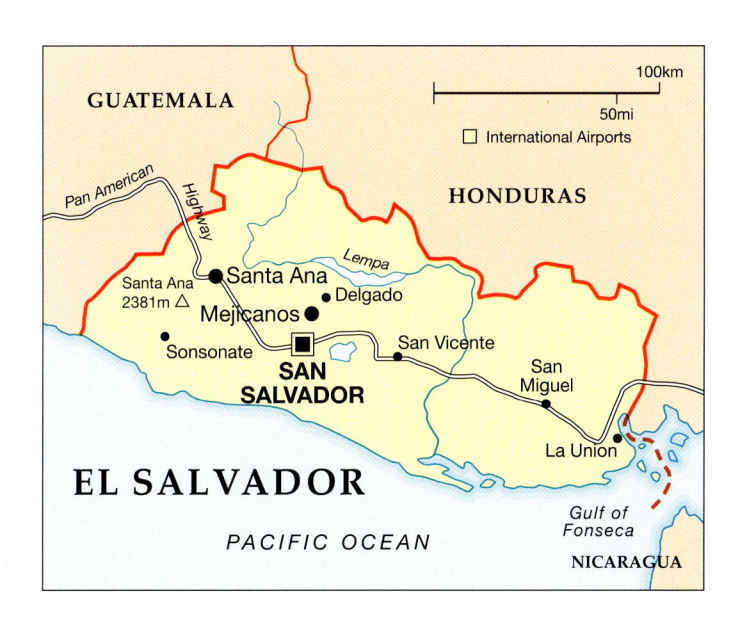

Facts and Figures

Capital: San Salvador 1,522,130 (1992)
Area (sq km): 21,041
Population: 5,050,000 (1992)
Language: Spanish
Religion: Roman Catholic 91%
 Protestant 4%
Currency: Colón = 100 centavos
Annual Income per person: $1,070
Annual Trade per person: $250
Adult Literacy: 73%
Life Expectancy (F): 69
Life Expectancy (M): 64

GREENLAND

Facts and Figures

Capital: Godthåb (Nuuk) 12,200 (1993)
Area (sq km): 2,175,600
Population: 55,000 (1993)
Language: Eskimo dialects, Danish
Religion: Evanjelical Lutherans 98%
Currency: Danish Krone = 100 ore
Annual Income per person: $6,000
Annual Trade per person: $15,017
Adult Literacy: Data not available
Life Expectancy (F): 69
Life Expectancy (M): 63

37

GRENADA

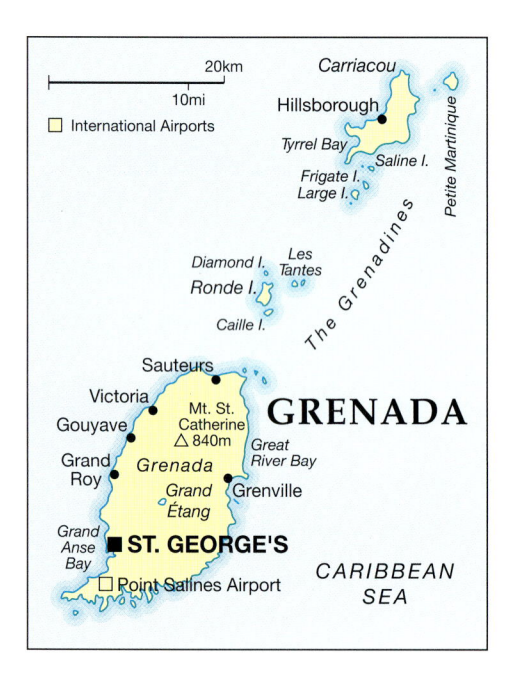

GUATEMALA

Facts and Figures

Capital: Guatemala City 2,000,000 (1989)
Area (sq km): 108,890
Population: 9,740,000 (1992)
Language: Spanish, Indian dialects
Religion: Roman Catholic 71%
　　　　　　Pentecostal 23%
　　　　　　Other Protestant 7%
Currency: Quetzal = 100 centavos
Annual Income per person: $930
Annual Trade per person: $286
Adult Literacy: 55%
Life Expectancy (F): 67
Life Expectancy (M): 62

Facts and Figures

Capital: St George's 35,750 (1980)
Area (sq km): 344
Population: 95,350 (1993)
Language: English, French patois
Religion: Roman Catholic 53% Anglican 14%
　　　　　　Seventh Day Adventist 9%
　　　　　　Pentecostal 7%
Currency: Eastern Caribbean $
Annual Income per person: $2,180
Annual Trade per person: $1,342
Adult Literacy: 96%
Life Expectancy (F): 74
Life Expectancy (M): 69

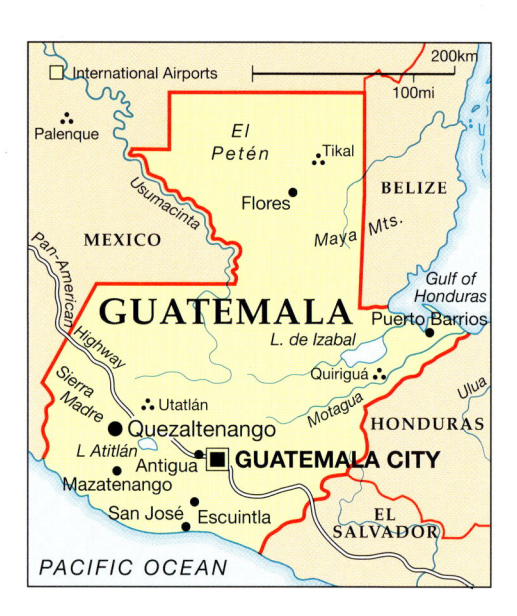

HAITI

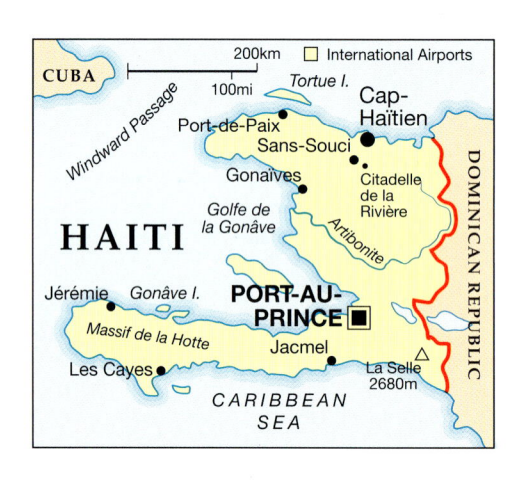

Facts and Figures

Capital: Port-au-Prince 1,402,000 (1991)
Area (sq km): 27,750
Population: 6,760,000 (1992)
Language: Haitian Créole, French
Religion: Roman Catholic 75% Other
　　　　　　Christian 10% Voodoo
Currency: Gourde = 100 centimes
Annual Income per person: $370
Annual Trade per person: $70
Adult Literacy: 53%
Life Expectancy (F): 58
Life Expectancy (M): 55

HONDURAS

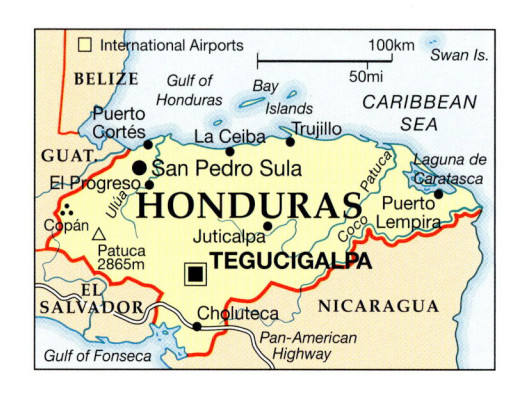

Facts and Figures

Capital: Tegucigalpa 678,700 (1988)
Area (sq km): 112,088
Population: 5,260,000
Language: Spanish
Religion: Roman Catholic 97%
Currency: Lempira = 100 centavos
Annual Income per person: $570
Annual Trade per person: $321
Adult Literacy: 73%
Life Expectancy (F): 68
Life Expectancy (M): 64

JAMAICA

Facts and Figures

Capital: Kingston 587.800 (1991)
Area (sq km): 11,425
Population: 2,450,000 (1992)
Language: English, English Creole
Religion: Protestant 70%
　　　　　Roman Catholic 8%
Currency: Jamaican Dollar $
Annual Income per person: $1,380
Annual Trade per person: $1,242
Adult Literacy: 98%
Life Expectancy (F): 76
Life Expectancy (M): 71

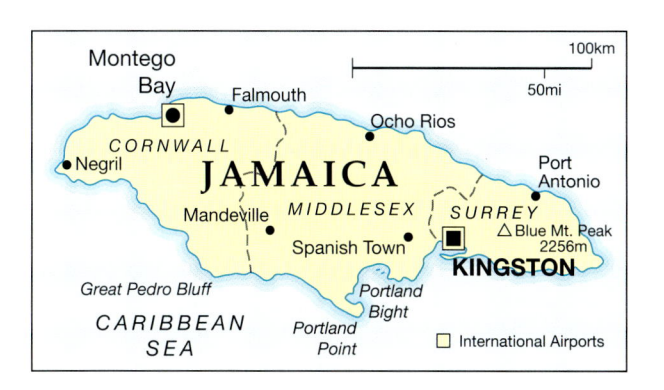

MEXICO

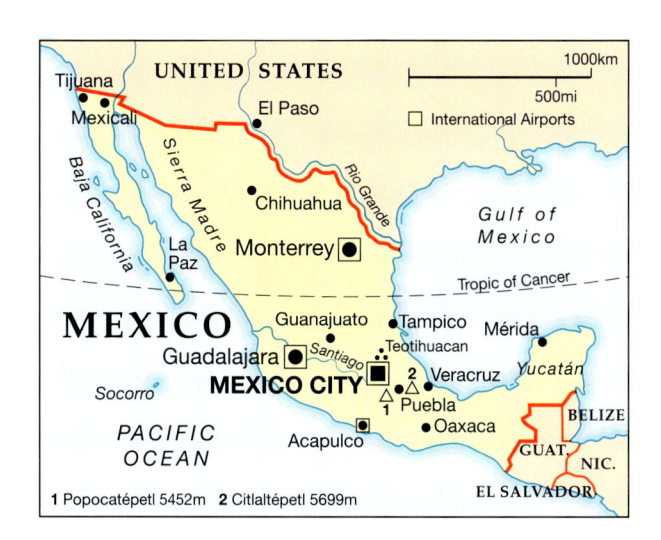

1 Popocatépetl 5452m　2 Citlaltépetl 5699m

Facts and Figures

Capital: Mexico City 15,047,770 (1990)
Area (sq km): 1,967,200
Population: 91,600,000 (1992)
Language: Spanish
Religion: Roman Catholic 94%
　　　　　Protestant 3%
Currency: Peso = 100 centavos
Annual Income per person: $2,870
Annual Trade per person: $743
Adult Literacy: 87%
Life Expectancy (F): 74
Life Expectancy (M): 67

NICARAGUA

Facts and Figures

Capital: Managua 682,100 (1985)
Area (sq km): 130,682
Population: 4,200,000 (1991)
Language: Spanish
Religion: Roman Catholic 88%
Currency: Córdoba = 100 centavos
Annual Income per person: $340
Annual Trade per person: $349
Adult Literacy: 81%
Life Expectancy (F): 68
Life Expectancy (M): 65

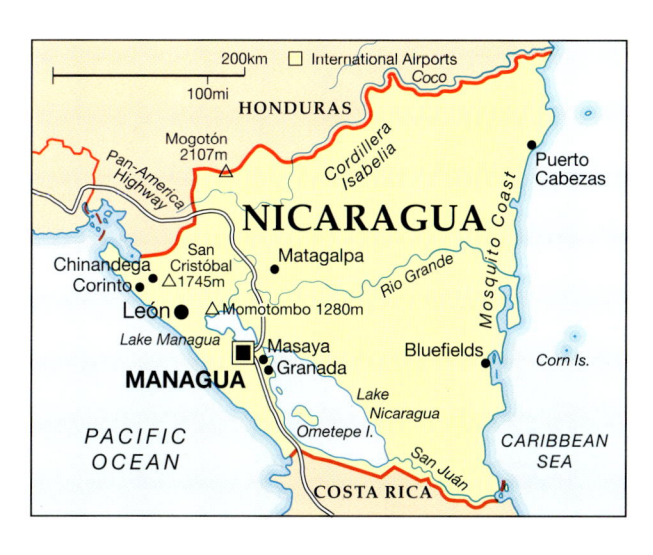

PANAMA

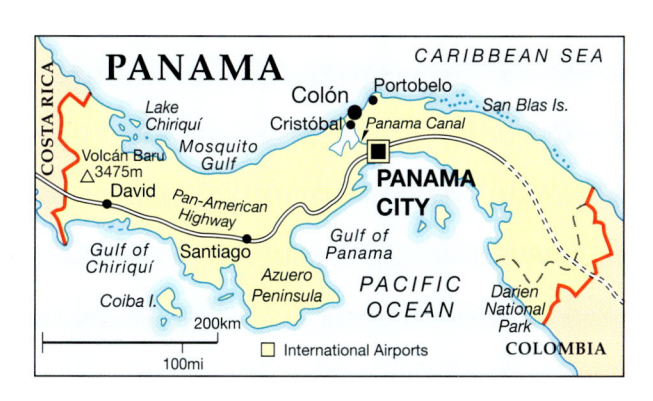

Facts and Figures

Capital: Panama City 584,800 (1990)
Area (sq km): 77,080
Population: 2,330,000 (1990)
Language: Spanish, English
Religion: Roman Catholic 85%
　　　　　Protestant 5% Moslem 5%
Currency: Balboa = 100 centesimos
Annual Income per person: $2180
Annual Trade per person: $825
Adult Literacy: 72%
Life Expectancy (F): 75
Life Expectancy (M): 71

39

PUERTO RICO

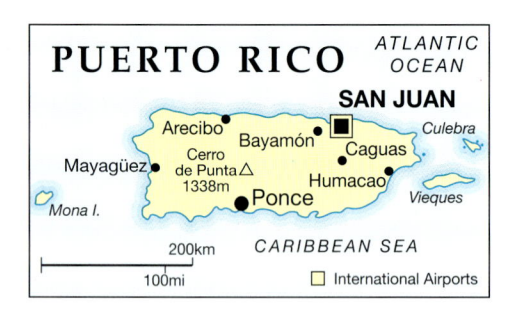

ST. CHRISTOPHER NEVIS

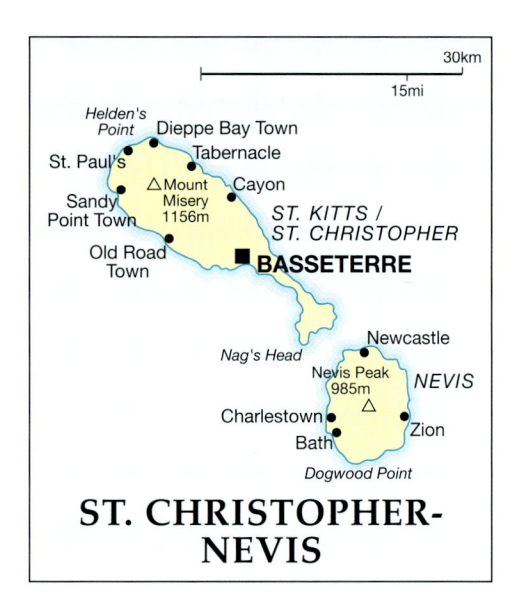

Facts and Figures

Capital: Basseterre 14,300 (1980)
Area (sq km): 262
Population: 40,620 (1991)
Language: English
Religion: Protestant 76%
 Roman Catholic 11%
Currency: East Caribbean Dollar
 =100cents
Annual Income per person: $3,960
Annual Trade per person: $3,200
Adult Literacy: 92%
Life Expectancy (F): 71
Life Expectancy (M): 64

Facts and Figures

Facts and Figures for Puerto Rico are incorporated into the details given for the United States of America

ST. LUCIA

Facts and Figures

Capital: Castries 53,900 (1992)
Area (sq km): 617
Population: 136,000 (1992)
Language: English, French patois
Religion: Roman Catholic 82%
 Protestant 10%
Currency: East Caribbean Dollar
 =100cents
Annual Income per person: $2,500
Annual Trade per person: $2,267
Adult Literacy: 93%
Life Expectancy (F): 74
Life Expectancy (M): 69

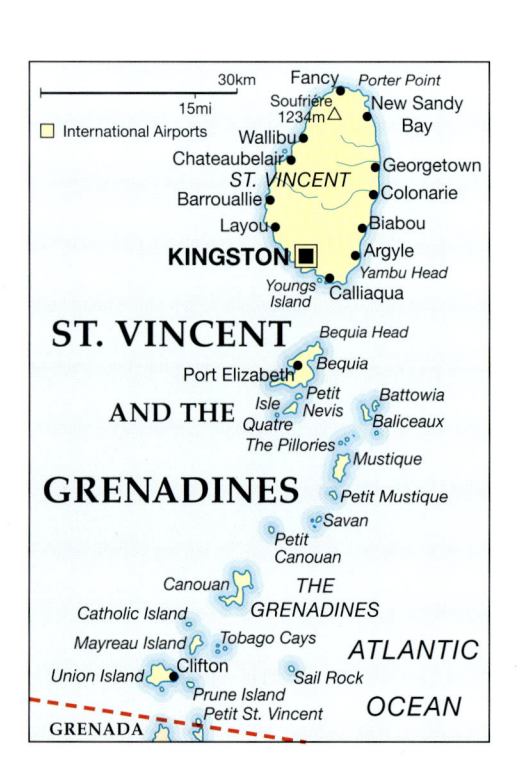

ST. VINCENT

Facts and Figures

Capital: Kingstown 26,600 (1991)
Area (sq km): 388
Population: 107,600 (1991)
Language: English, French patois
Religion: Protestant 53%
 Roman Catholic 12%
Currency: E. Carib. Dollar =100 cents
Annual Income per person: $1,730
Annual Trade per person: $1,800
Adult Literacy: 84%
Life Expectancy (F): 72
Life Expectancy (M): 68

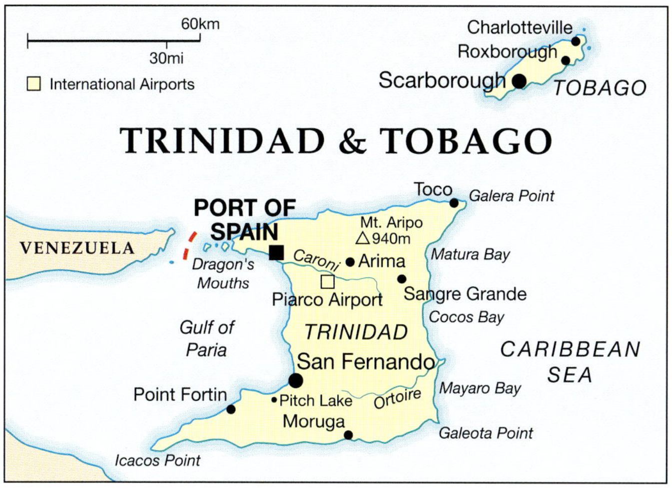

TRINIDAD & TOBAGO

Facts and Figures

Capital: Port-of-Spain 58,400 (1990)
Area (sq km): 5,124
Population: 1,250,000 (1991)
Language: English
Religion: Roman Catholic 29% Protestant 11% Hindu 24% Muslim 6%
Currency: Trinidad and Tobago $ =100 cents
Annual Income per person: $3,620
Annual Trade per person: $2,902
Adult Literacy: 96%
Life Expectancy (F): 75
Life Expectancy (M): 70

UNITED STATES OF AMERICA

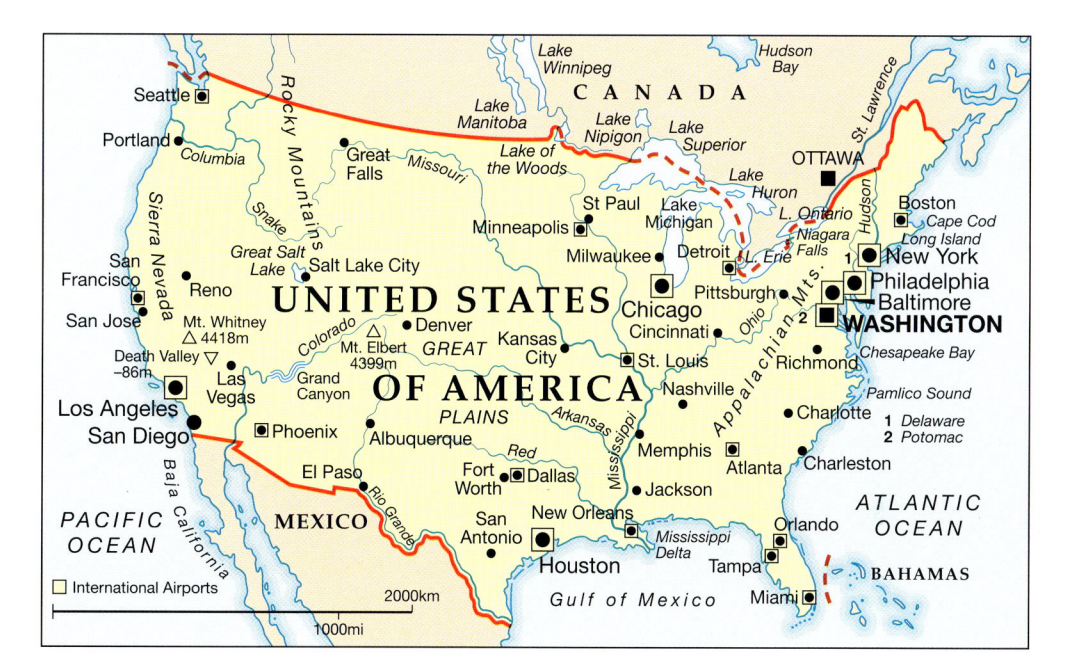

Facts and Figures

Capital: Washington D. C. 606,900 (1990)
Area (sq km): 9,158,960
Population: 252,180,000 (1991)
Language: English, Spanish
Religion: Christian, Jewish
Currency: US Dollar = 100 cents
Annual Income per person: $22,560
Annual Trade per person: $3,922
Adult Literacy: 99%
Life Expectancy (F): 79
Life Expectancy (M): 72

US States

1 NEW HAMPSHIRE
2 VERMONT
3 MASSACHUSETTS
4 RHODE ISLAND
5 CONNECTICUT
6 DELAWARE
7 MARYLAND
8 WEST VIRGINIA

41

South America

South America

COUNTRY	PAGE
Argentina	44
Bolivia	44
Brazil	44
Chile	45
Colombia	45
Ecuador	45
Guyana	46
Paraguay	46
Peru	46
Surinam	47
Uruguay	47
Venezuela	47

ARGENTINA

Facts and Figures

Capital: Buenos Aires 9,927,400 (1980)
Area (sq km): 2,780,092
Population: 32,370,000 (1991)
Language: Spanish
Religion: Roman Catholic 94%
Protestant 2%
Currency: Peso
Annual Income per person: $2,780
Annual Trade per person: $613
Adult Literacy: 95%
Life Expectancy (F): 75
Life Expectancy (M): 68

BOLIVIA

Facts and Figures

Capital: Sucre 105,800 (1988)
Area (sq km): 1,098,580
Population: 7,610,000 (1991)
Language: Spanish, Aymara, Quechua
Religion: Roman Catholic 89%
Currency: Boliviano = 100 centavos
Annual Income per person: $650
Annual Trade per person: $237
Adult Literacy: 78%
Life Expectancy (F): 58
Life Expectancy (M): 54

BRAZIL

Facts and Figures

Capital: Brasilia 1,596,270 (1991)
Area (sq km): 8,511,996
Population: 159,100,000 (1991)
Language: Portuguese, Spanish, English
Religion: Roman Catholic 89%
Protestant 7%
Currency: Cruzeiro Real = 100 centavos
Annual Income per person: $2,920
Annual Trade per person: $343
Adult Literacy: 81%
Life Expectancy (F): 69
Life Expectancy (M): 64

44

CHILE

Facts and Figures

Capital: Santiago 4,858,350 (1987)
Area (sq km): 736,900
Population: 13,440,000 (1993)
Language: Spanish
Religion: Roman Catholic 80%
Protestant 6%
Currency: Chilean Peso = 100 centavos
Annual Income per person: $2,160
Annual Trade per person: $1,221
Adult Literacy: 93%
Life Expectancy (F): 76
Life Expectancy (M): 69

COLOMBIA

Facts and Figures

Capital: Bogotá 4,921,300 (1992)
Area (sq km): 1,141,750
Population: 33,390,000 (1992)
Language: Spanish
Religion: Roman Catholic 94%
Currency: Colombian Peso = 100 centavos
Annual Income per person: $1,280
Annual Trade per person: $364
Adult Literacy: 87%
Life Expectancy (F): 72
Life Expectancy (M): 66

ECUADOR

Facts and Figures

Capital: Quito 1,100,850 (1990)
Area (sq km): 272,045
Population: 9,650,000 (1990)
Language: Spanish, Quechua
Religion: Roman Catholic 91%
Protestant 6%
Currency: Sucre = 100 centavos
Annual Income per person: $1,020
Annual Trade per person: $474
Adult Literacy: 86%
Life Expectancy (F): 69
Life Expectancy (M): 65

GUYANA

Facts and Figures

Capital: Georgetown 188,000 (1983)
Area (sq km): 214,970
Population: 990,000 (1989)
Language: English, Hindi, Urdu
Religion: Protestant 34% Hindu 34%
Roman Catholic 18% Muslim 9%
Currency: Guyanan Dollar = 100 cents
Annual Income per person: $290
Annual Trade per person: $959
Adult Literacy: 96%
Life Expectancy (F): 68
Life Expectancy (M): 62

PARAGUAY

Facts and Figures

Capital: Asunción 607,700 (1990)
Area (sq km): 406,750
Population: 4,500,000 (1993)
Language: Spanish, Guaraní
Religion: Roman Catholic 96%
Currency: Guaraní = 100 céntimos
Annual Income per person: $1,210
Annual Trade per person: $447
Adult Literacy: 90%
Life Expectancy (F): 70
Life Expectancy (M): 65

PERU

Facts and Figures

Capital: Lima 5,759,700 (1993)
Area (sq km): 1,244,300
Population: 22,130,000 (1993)
Language: Spanish, Quechua, Aymara
Religion: Roman Catholic 93%
Currency: Nuevo sol = 100 centavos
Annual Income per person: $1,020
Annual Trade per person: $288
Adult Literacy: 85%
Life Expectancy (F): 67
Life Expectancy (M): 63

SURINAM

Facts and Figures

Capital: Paramaribo 201,000 (1993)
Area (sq km): 163,820
Population: 404,310 (1991)
Language: Dutch, Spanish, English
Religion: Hindu 24% Roman Catholic 20% Muslim 17% Protestant 16% Other 7%
Currency: Surinam Guilder = 100 cents
Annual Income per person: $3,610
Annual Trade per person: $2,100
Adult Literacy: 95%
Life Expectancy (F): 73
Life Expectancy (M): 68

URUGUAY

Facts and Figures

Capital: Montevideo 1,383,700 (1992)
Area (sq km): 176,215
Population: 3,120,000 (1992)
Language: Spanish
Religion: Roman Catholic 56%
Currency: Uruguayan peso = 100 centésimos
Annual Income per person: $2,860
Annual Trade per person: $1,032
Adult Literacy: 96%
Life Expectancy (F): 76
Life Expectancy (M): 69

VENEZUELA

Facts and Figures

Capital: Caracas 1,044,900 (1981)
Area (sq km): 912,050
Population: 20,410,000 (1993)
Language: Spanish
Religion: Roman Catholic 86%
Currency: Bolívar = 100 céntimos
Annual Income per person: $2,610
Annual Trade per person: $1,288
Adult Literacy: 88%
Life Expectancy (F): 74
Life Expectancy (M): 67

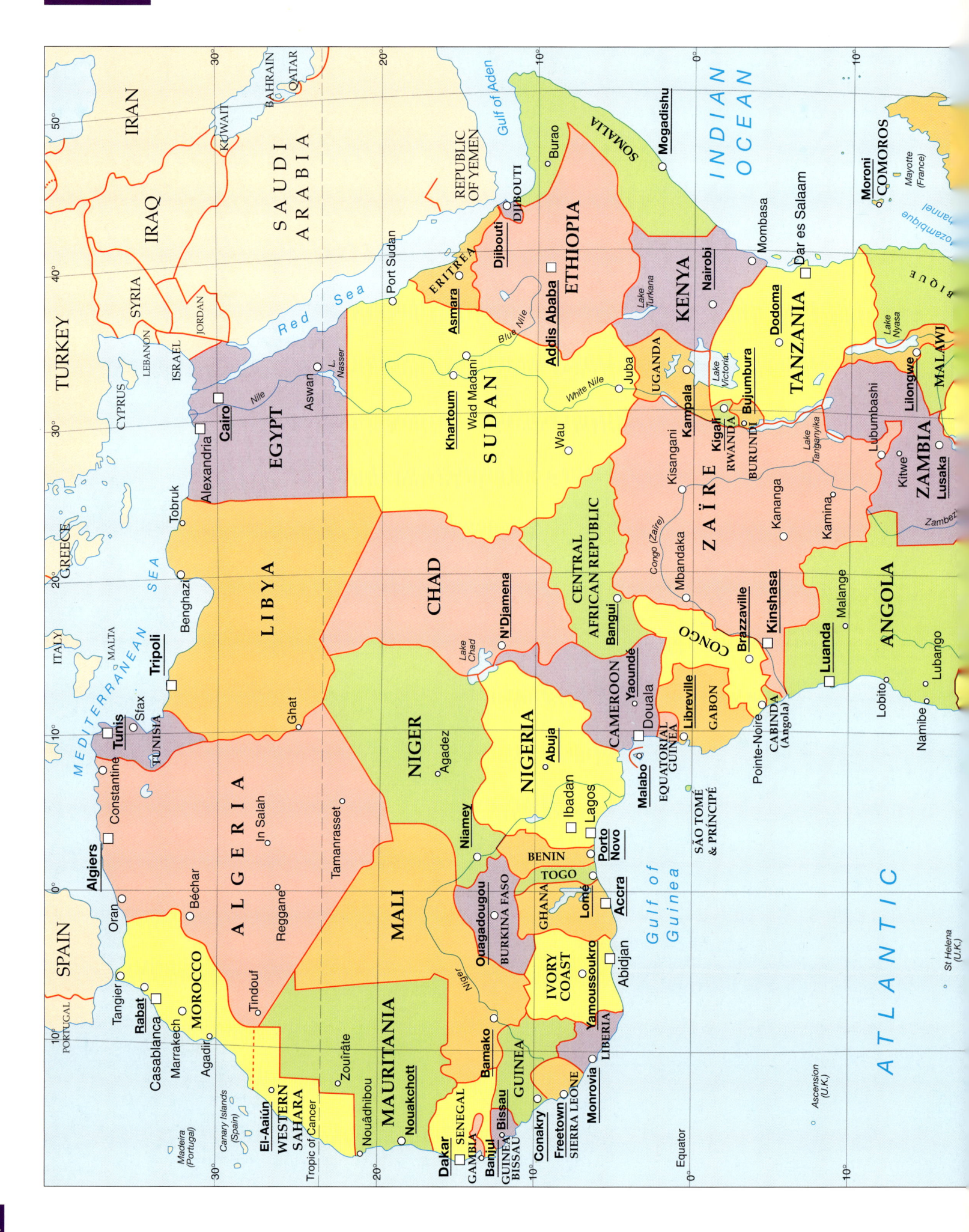

AFRICA

AFRICA

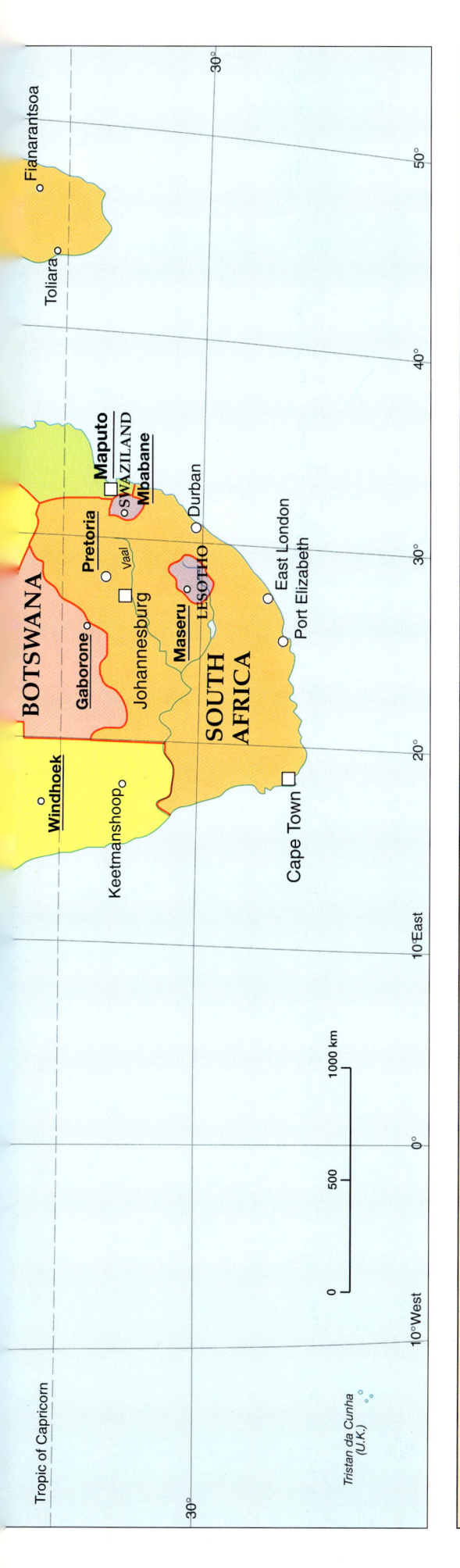

COUNTRY	PAGE	COUNTRY	PAGE
Algeria	50	Mauritania	60
Angola	50	Mauritius	60
Azores	50	Morocco	61
Benin	51	Mozambique	61
Botswana	51	Namibia	61
Burkina Faso	51	Niger	62
Burundi	52	Nigeria	62
Cameroon	52	Rwanda	62
Canary Islands	52	São Tomé & Príncipe	63
Cape Verde	53	Senegal	63
Central African Republic	53	Seychelles	63
Chad	53	Sierra Leone	63
Comoros	54	Somalia	64
Congo	54	South Africa	64
Cote d'Ivoire	54	Sudan	64
Djibouti	54	Swaziland	65
Egypt	55	Tanzania	65
Eritrea	55	Togo	65
Ethiopia	55	Tunisia	66
Equatorial Guinea	55	Uganda	66
Gabon	56	Zaire	66
Gambia	56	Zambia	67
Ghana	56	Zimbabwe	67
Guinea	57		
Guinea Bissau	57		
Kenya	57		
Lesotho	58		
Liberia	58		
Libya	58		
Madagascar	59		
Madeira	59		
Malawi	59		
Mali	60		

ALGERIA

Facts and Figures

Capital: Algiers 1,507,000 (1987)
Area (sq km): 2,381,741
Population: 26,600,000 (1993)
Language: Arabic, French, Berber
Religion: Sunni Muslim 98%
Currency: Algerian Dinar = 100 centimes
Annual Income per person: $2,020
Annual Trade per person: $639
Adult Literacy: 57%
Life Expectancy (F): 67
Life Expectancy (M): 65

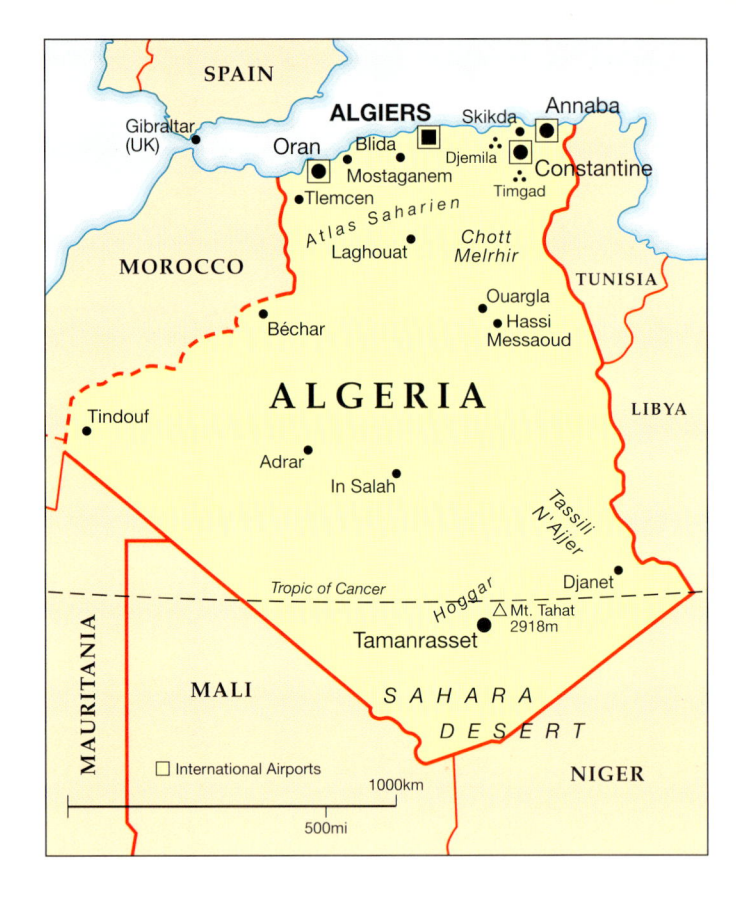

ANGOLA

Facts and Figures

Capital: Luanda 480,600 (1988)
Area (sq km): 1,246,700
Population: 10,770,000 (1993)
Language: Portuguese
Religion: Roman Catholic 75% Protestant 13% Traditional 16%
Currency: Kwanza = 100 lwei
Annual Income per person: $620
Annual Trade per person: $281
Adult Literacy: 42%
Life Expectancy (F): 48
Life Expectancy (M): 45

AZORES

Facts and Figures

Capital: Ponta Delgada 21,091 (1991)
Area (sq km): 2,247
Population: 260,000 (1991)
Language: Portuguese
Religion: Roman Catholic
Currency: Escudo
Annual Income per person: N/A
Annual Trade per person: N/A
Adult Literacy: N/A
Life Expectancy (F): N/A
Life Expectancy (M): N/A

BENIN.

Facts and Figures

Capital: Porto Novo 208,260 (1982)
Area (sq km): 112,620
Population: 5,010,000 (1993)
Language: French, Fon
Religion: Traditional 60% Roman Catholic 18% Sunni Muslim 15%
Currency: CFA Franc = 100 centimes
Annual Income per person: $380
Annual Trade per person: $156
Adult Literacy: 23%
Life Expectancy (F): 50
Life Expectancy (M): 46

BOTSWANA

Facts and Figures

Capital: Gaborone 138,470 (1991)
Area (sq km): 581,730
Population: 1,330,000 (1991)
Language: English, Setswana
Religion: Traditional 50% Christian 30%
Currency: Pula = 100 thebe
Annual Income per person: $2,590
Annual Trade per person: $2,500
Adult Literacy: 74%
Life Expectancy (F): 64
Life Expectancy (M): 58

BURKINA FASO

Facts and Figures

Capital: Ouagadougou 442,230 (1985)
Area (sq km): 274,400
Population: 9,190,000 (1991)
Language: French
Religion: Sunni Muslim 52% Christian 21%
Currency: CFA Franc = 100 centimes
Annual Income per person: $350
Annual Trade per person: $48
Adult Literacy: 18%
Life Expectancy (F): 51
Life Expectancy (M): 48

BURUNDI

Facts and Figures

Capital: Bujumbura 241,000 (1989)
Area (sq km): 27,830
Population: 5,600,000 (1992)
Language: French, Kirundi
Religion: Roman Catholic 62%
  Traditional 30%
Currency: Burundi Franc = 100 centimes
Annual Income per person: $210
Annual Trade per person: $60
Adult Literacy: 50%
Life Expectancy (F): 51
Life Expectancy (M): 48

CAMEROON

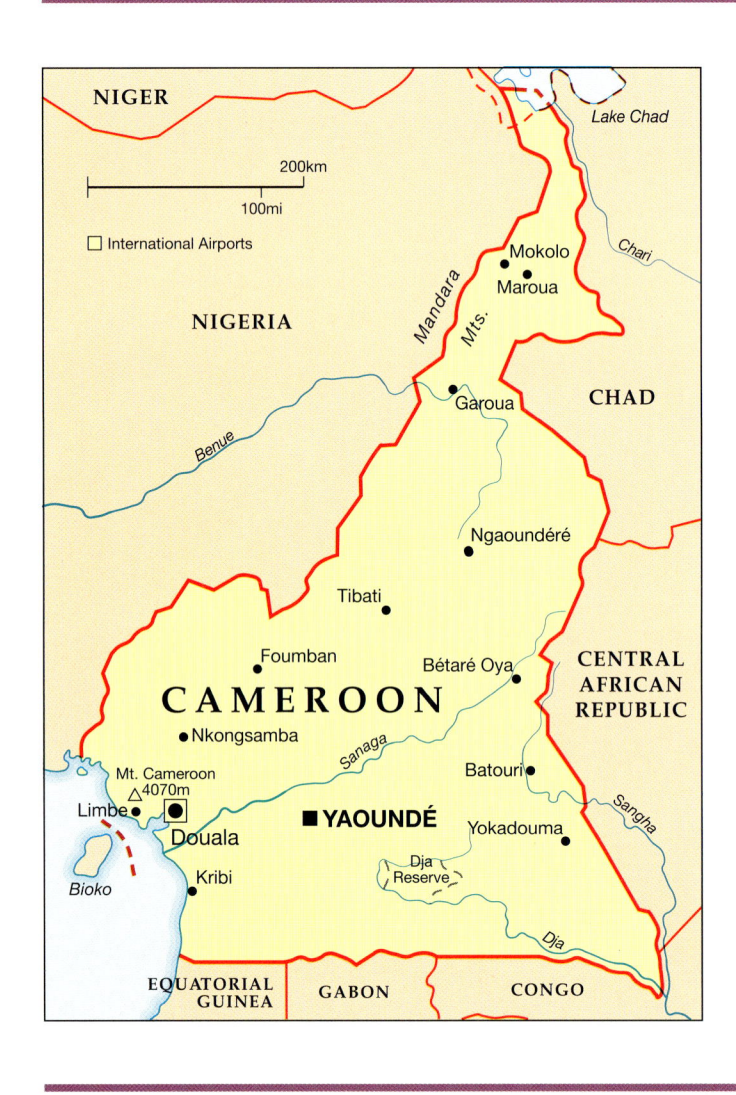

Facts and Figures

Capital: Yaoundé 750,000 (1991)
Area (sq km): 475,442
Population: 12,240,000 (1991)
Language: French, English
Religion: Roman Catholic 28%
  Animist 25% Sunni Muslim 22%
  Protestant 18%
Currency: CFA Franc = 100 centimes
Annual Income per person: $940
Annual Trade per person: $310
Adult Literacy: 54%
Life Expectancy (F): 57
Life Expectancy (M): 54

CANARY ISLANDS

Facts and Figures

Facts and Figures for CANARY ISLANDS are incorporated with SPAIN

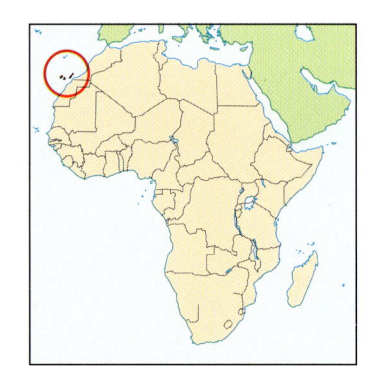

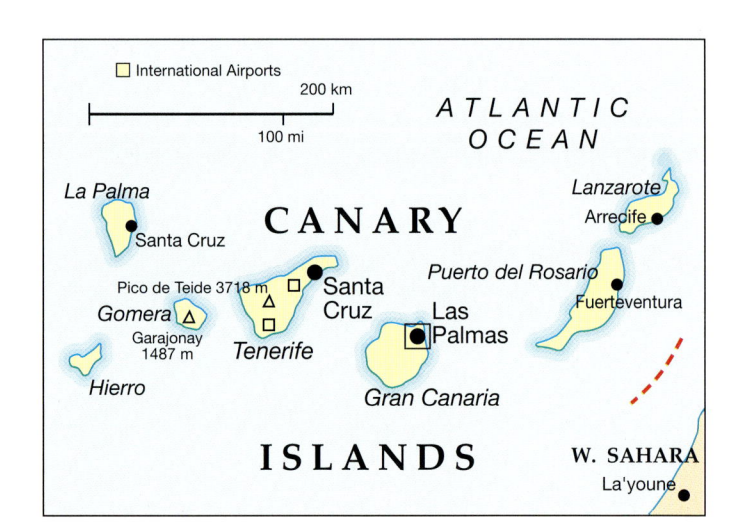

52

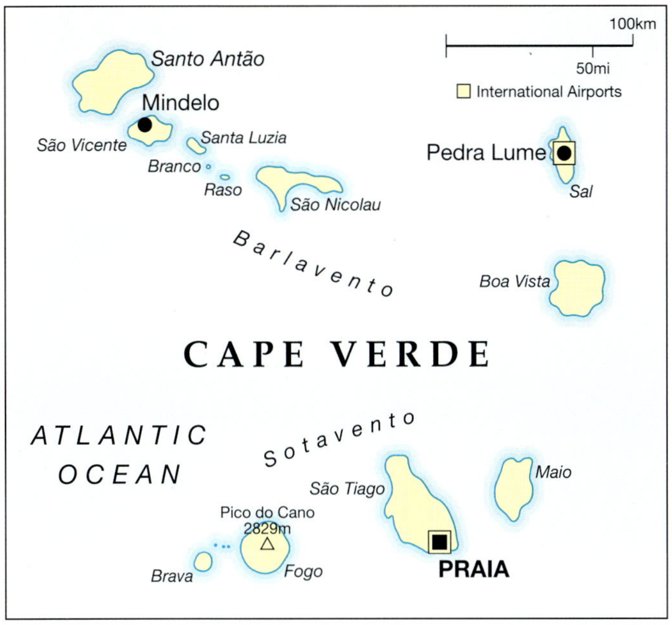

CAPE VERDE

Facts and Figures

Capital: Praia 61,700 (1990)
Area (sq km): 4,030
Population: 350,000 (1993)
Language: Portuguese, Crioulo
Religion: Roman Catholic 93%
Protestant 7%
Currency: Escudo = 100 centavos
Annual Income per person: $750
Annual Trade per person: $331
Adult Literacy: 53 %
Life Expectancy (F): 69
Life Expectancy (M): 67

CENTRAL AFRICAN REPUBLIC

Facts and Figures

Capital: Bangui 451,700 (1988)
Area (sq km): 622,440
Population: 3,130,000 (1991)
Language: French, Sango
Religion: Protestant 45% RC 30%
Traditional
Currency: CFA Franc = 100 centimes
Annual Income per person: $390
Annual Trade per person: $70
Adult Literacy: 38%
Life Expectancy (F): 53
Life Expectancy (M): 48

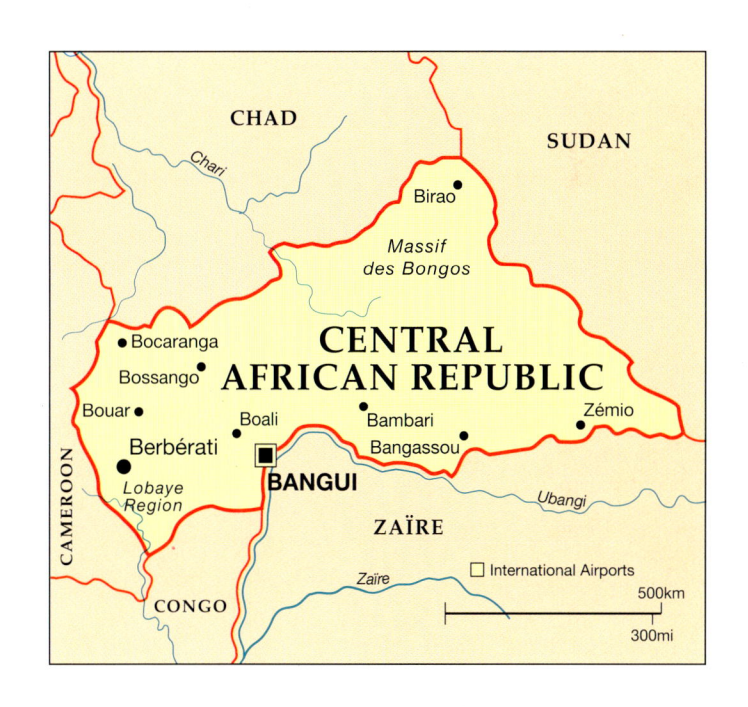

CHAD

Facts and Figures

Capital: N'Djaména 529,560 (1993)
Area (sq km): 1,284,000
Population: 6,290,000 (1993)
Language: French, Arabic
Religion: Muslim 41% Traditional 35%
Christian 23%
Currency: CFA Franc = 100 centimes
Annual Income per person: $220
Annual Trade per person: $104
Adult Literacy: 30%
Life Expectancy (F): 49
Life Expectancy (M): 46

COMOROS

Facts and Figures

Capital: Moroni 22,000 (1992)
Area (sq km): 2,230
Population: 510,000 (1992)
Language: Swahili, French, Arabic
Religion: Sunni Muslim 93%
Currency: Comorian Franc
Annual Income per person: $500
Annual Trade per person: $120
Adult Literacy: 61%
Life Expectancy (F): 57
Life Expectancy (M): 56

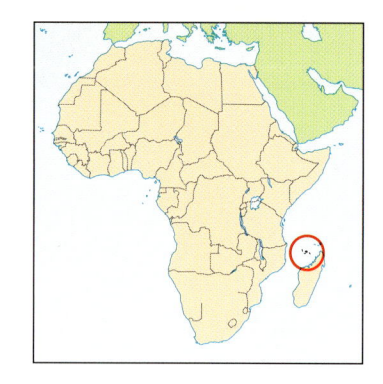

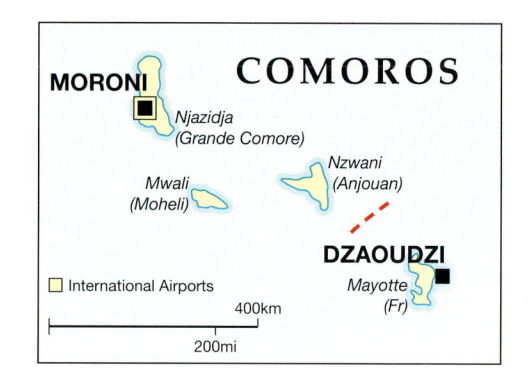

CONGO

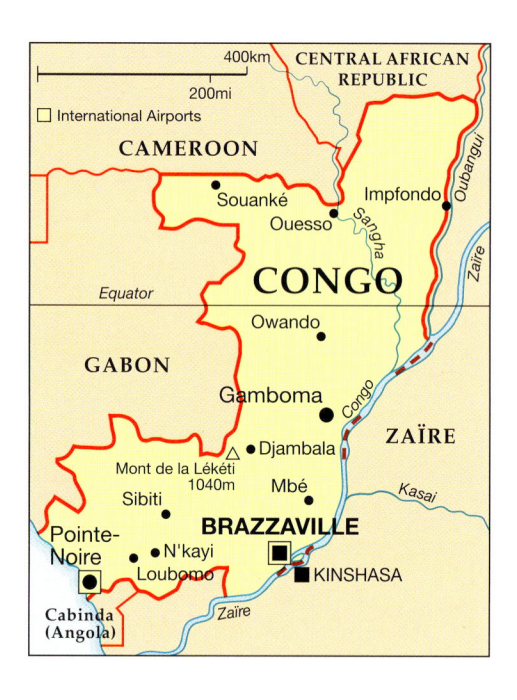

COTE D'IVOIRE

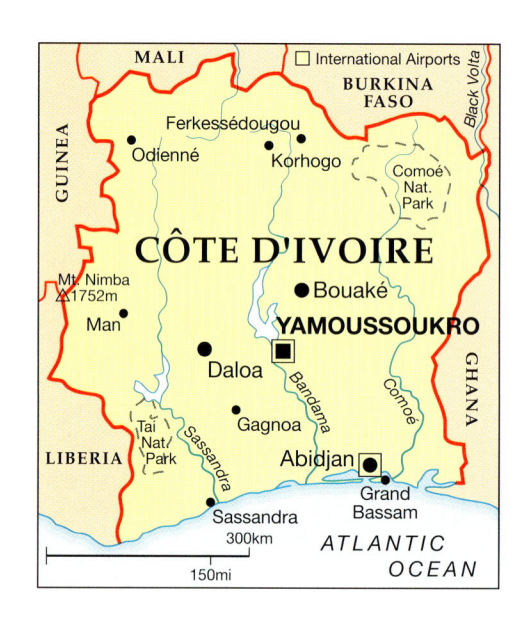

Facts and Figures

Capital: Yamoussoukro 120,000 (1986)
Area (sq km): 322,460
Population: 13,100,000 (1991)
Language: French
Religion: Muslim 20% RC 20% Traditional 44%
Currency: CFA Franc = 100 centimes
Annual Income per person: $690
Annual Trade per person: $443
Adult Literacy: 54%
Life Expectancy (F): 56
Life Expectancy (M): 53

DJIBOUTI

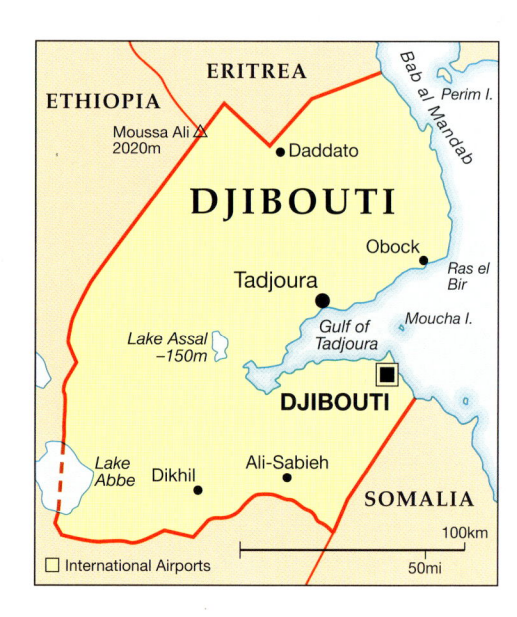

Facts and Figures

Capital: Brazzaville 937,600 (1992)
Area (sq km): 341,800
Population: 2,690,000 (1992)
Language: French
Religion: Roman Catholic 46% Protestant 19% Traditional
Currency: CFA Franc = 100 centimes
Annual Income per person: $1,120
Annual Trade per person: $694
Adult Literacy: 57%
Life Expectancy (F): 57
Life Expectancy (M): 52

Facts and Figures

Capital: Djibouti 317,000 (1991)
Area (sq km): 23,200
Population: 542,000 (1991)
Language: Arabic, French, Cushitic
Religion: Sunni Muslim 94% Roman Catholic 4%
Currency: Djibouti Franc
Annual Income per person: $1,000
Annual Trade per person: $550
Adult Literacy: 19%
Life Expectancy (F): 51
Life Expectancy (M): 47

EGYPT

Facts and Figures

Capital: Cairo 6,663,000 (1991)
Area (sq km): 1,001,450
Population: 56,430,000 (1993)
Language: Arabic, French, English
Religion: Sunni Muslim 92% Christian
Currency: Egyptian Pound = 100 piastres
Annual Income per person: $620
Annual Trade per person: $211
Adult Literacy: 48%
Life Expectancy (F): 63
Life Expectancy (M): 60

EQUATORIAL GUINEA

Facts and Figures

Capital: Malabo 370,000 (1988)
Area (sq km): 28,051
Population: 417,000 (1990)
Language: Spanish, Fang
Religion: Roman Catholic 89%
Currency: CFA Franc = 100 centimes
Annual Income per person: $330
Annual Trade per person: $250
Adult Literacy: 50%
Life Expectancy (F): 50
Life Expectancy (M): 46

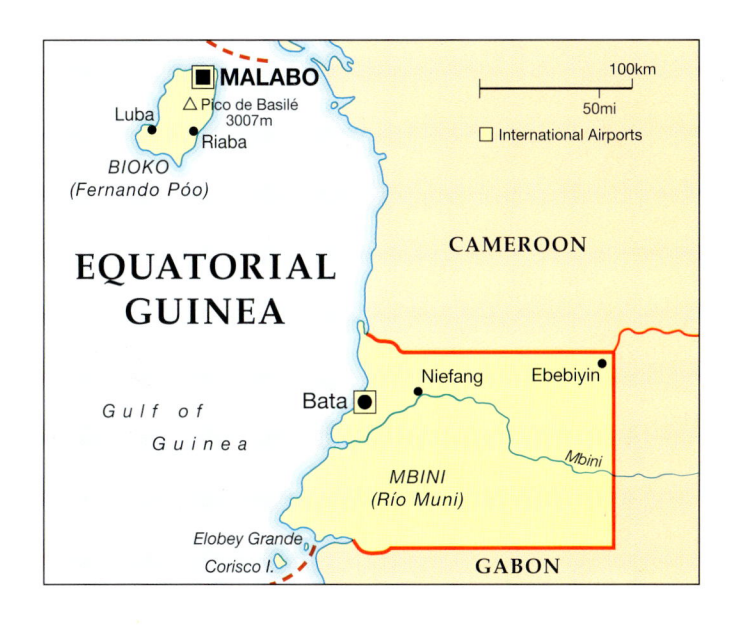

ERITREA & ETHIOPIA

Facts and Figures

ETHIOPIA
Capital: Addis Ababa 1,700,000 (1990)
Area (sq km): 1,157,603
Population: 51,980,000 (1993)
Language: Amharic, Galla, Tigre
Religion: Muslim 45%, Christian 40%, Traditional 12%
Currency: Ethiopian birr = 100 cents
Annual Income per person: $120
Annual Trade per person: $12
Adult Literacy: 66%
Life Expectancy (F): 49
Life Expectancy (M): 45

Facts and Figures

ERITREA
Capital: Asmara 367,300 (1991)
Area (sq km): 93,679
Population: 3,500,00 (1991)
Language: Tigrinya
Religion: Muslim 50% Coptic Christian 50%
Currency: Ethiopian birr = 100 cents
Annual Income per person: N/A
Annual Trade per person: N/A
Adult Literacy: N/A
Life Expectancy (F): N/A
Life Expectancy (M): N/A

GABON

Facts and Figures

Capital: Libreville 350,000 (1983)
Area (sq km): 267,670
Population: 1,010,000 (1993)
Language: French, Bantu
Religion: Roman Catholic 75%, Traditional
Currency: CFA Franc = 100 centimes
Annual Income per person: $3,780
Annual Trade per person: $2,094
Adult Literacy: 61%
Life Expectancy (F): 55
Life Expectancy (M): 52

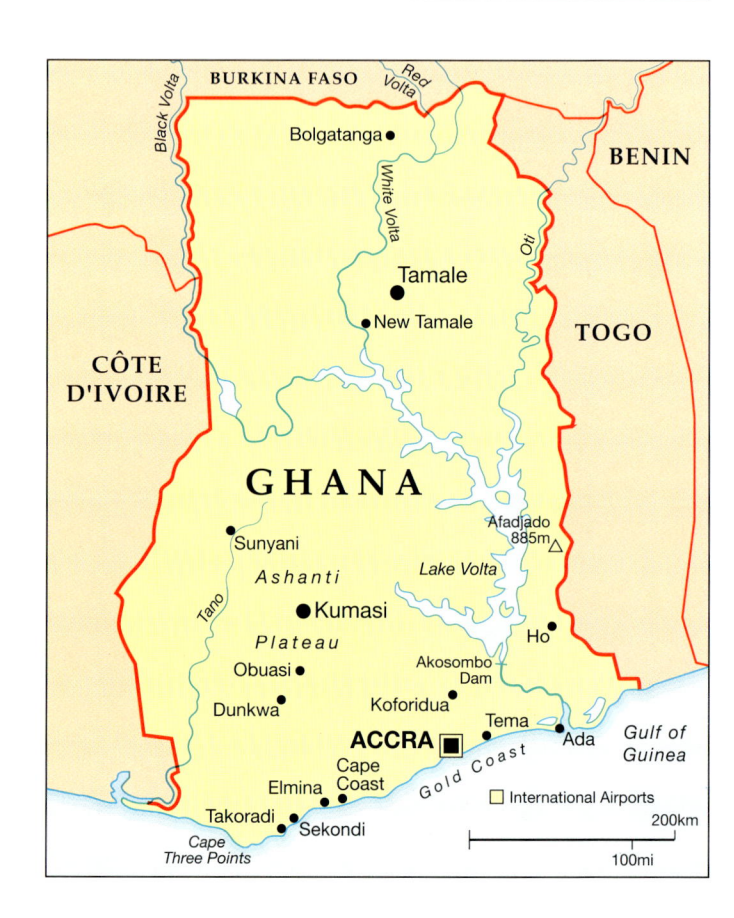

GAMBIA

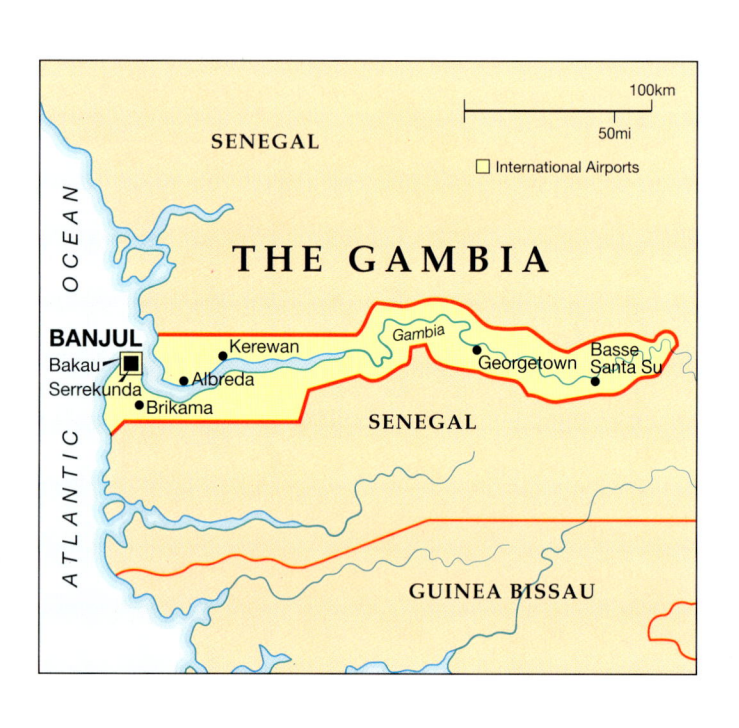

GHANA

Facts and Figures

Capital: Banjul 52,000 (1992)
Area (sq km): 11,300
Population: 875,000 (1990)
Language: English, Madinka
Religion: Sunni Muslim 95%, Christian 4%
Currency: Dalasi = 100 butut
Annual Income per person: $360
Annual Trade per person: $298
Adult Literacy: 27%
Life Expectancy (F): 47
Life Expectancy (M): 43

Facts and Figures

Capital: Accra 1,050,000 (1992)
Area (sq km): 238,540
Population: 16,700,000 (1991)
Language: English, Akan, Mossi, Ewe, Ga-Adangme
Religion: Protestant 28% Traditional 21% RC 19% Muslim 16%
Currency: Cedi = 100 pesewas
Annual Income per person: $400
Annual Trade per person: $158
Adult Literacy: 60%
Life Expectancy (F): 58
Life Expectancy (M): 54

GUINEA

Facts and Figures

Capital: Conakry 860,000 (1992)
Area (sq km): 245,860
Population: 7,300,000 (1990)
Language: French, Susu, Fulani, Malinké
Religion: Muslim 69% Traditional 30%
Currency: Guinean Franc = 100 cauris
Annual Income per person: $450
Annual Trade per person: $160
Adult Literacy: 24%
Life Expectancy (F): 45
Life Expectancy (M): 44

GUINEA BISSAU

Facts and Figures

Capital: Bissau 135,000 (1992)
Area (sq km): 36,125
Population: 980,000 (1991)
Language: Portuguese, Crioulo
Religion: Traditional 65% Muslim 30%
Currency: Peso = 100 centavos
Annual Income per person: $190
Annual Trade per person: $85
Adult Literacy: 36%
Life Expectancy (F): 45
Life Expectancy (M): 42

KENYA

Facts and Figures

Capital: Nairobi 1,500,000 (1992)
Area (sq km): 582,650
Population: 27,900,000 (1991)
Language: Swahili, Kikuyu, English
Religion: Roman Catholic 23%
Other Christian 23%
Protestant 15% Traditional 15%
Currency: Kenya shilling = 100 cents
Annual Income per person: $340
Annual Trade per person: $113
Adult Literacy: 69%
Life Expectancy (F): 63
Life Expectancy (M): 59

57

LESOTHO

Facts and Figures

Capital: Maseru 126,000 (1992)
Area (sq km): 30,355
Population: 1,830,000 (1991)
Language: Sesotho, English
Religion: Protestant 49%
 Roman Catholic 44%
Currency: Loti = 100 lisente
Annual Income per person: $580
Annual Trade per person: $350
Adult Literacy: 60%
Life Expectancy (F): 63
Life Expectancy (M): 54

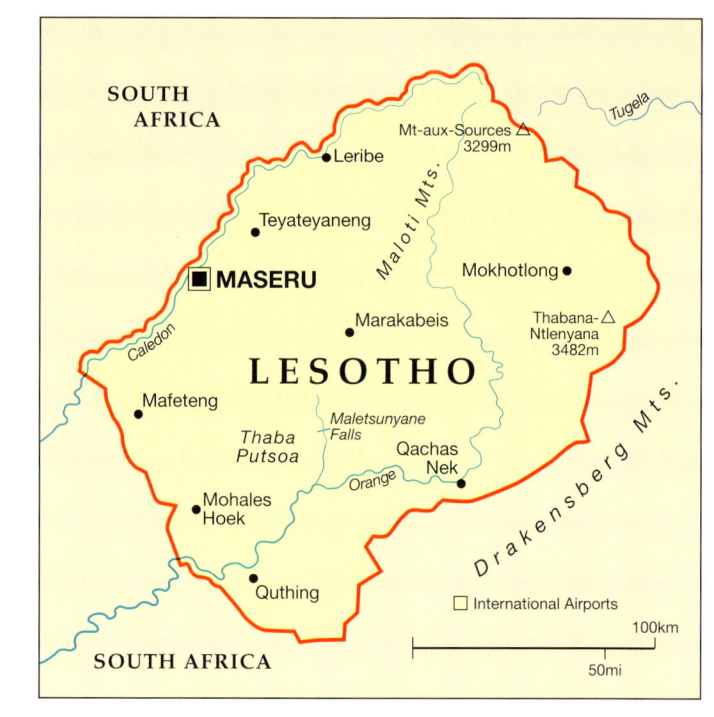

LIBERIA

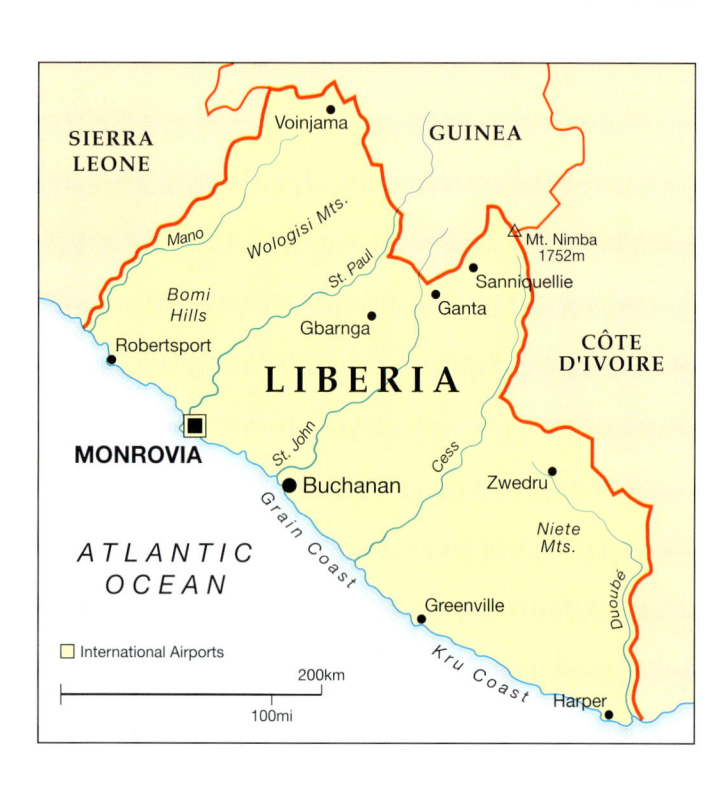

LIBYA

Facts and Figures

Capital: Tripoli 858,000 (1981)
Area (sq km): 1,759,540
Population: 4,700,000 (1990)
Language: Arabic, Berber
Religion: Sunni Muslim 97%
Currency: Libyan dinar = 1000 millemes
Annual Income per person: $5,500
Annual Trade per person: $3,332
Adult Literacy: 64%
Life Expectancy (F): 65
Life Expectancy (M): 62

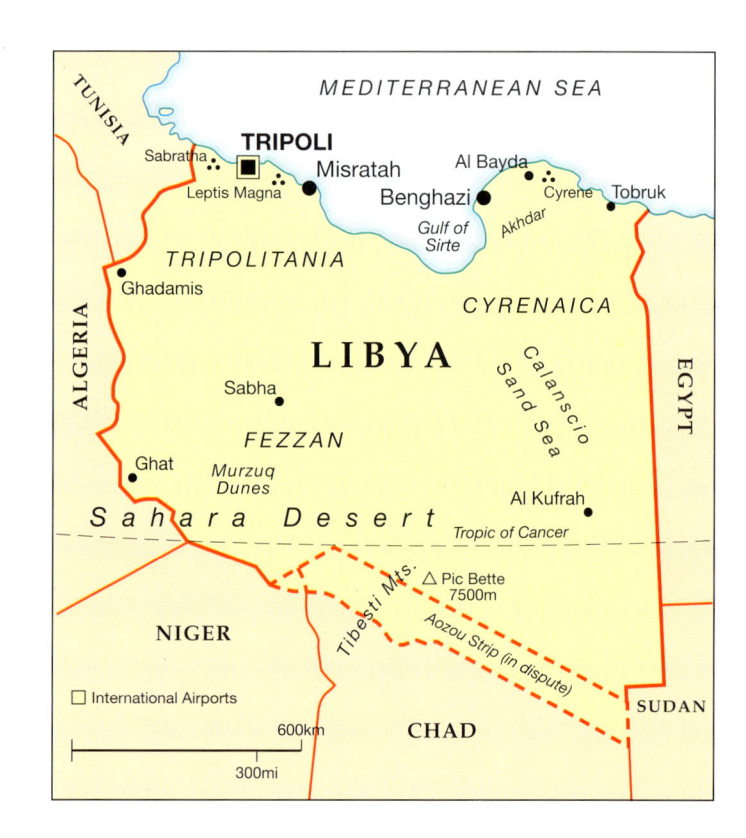

Facts and Figures

Capital: Monrovia 540,000 (1992)
Area (sq km): 99,070
Population: 2,830,000 (1992)
Language: English, Mande,
 West Atlantic, Kwa
Religion: Sunni Muslim 30%
 Protestant 15%
 Roman Catholic 5%
Currency: Liberian Dollar
Annual Income per person: $600
Annual Trade per person: $285
Adult Literacy: 40%
Life Expectancy (F): 57
Life Expectancy (M): 54

MADAGASCAR

Facts and Figures

Capital: Antananarivo 1,803,390 (1990)
Area (sq km): 587,040
Population: 12,370,000 (1991)
Language: Malagasy, French, English
Religion: Traditional 47% RC 26% Protestant 22%
Currency: Malagasy Franc = 100 centimes
Annual Income per person: $210
Annual Trade per person: $65
Adult Literacy: 80%
Life Expectancy (F): 57
Life Expectancy (M): 54

MADEIRA

Facts and Figures

Facts and Figures for MADEIRA are incorporated with PORTUGAL

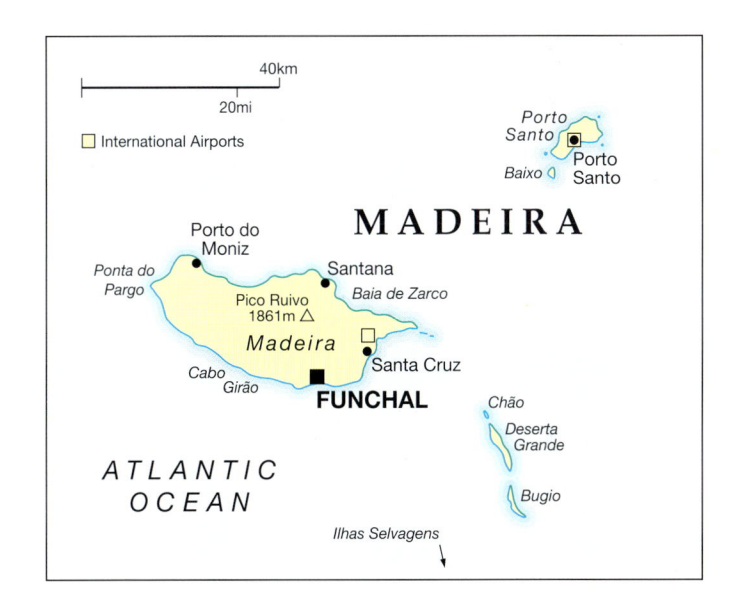

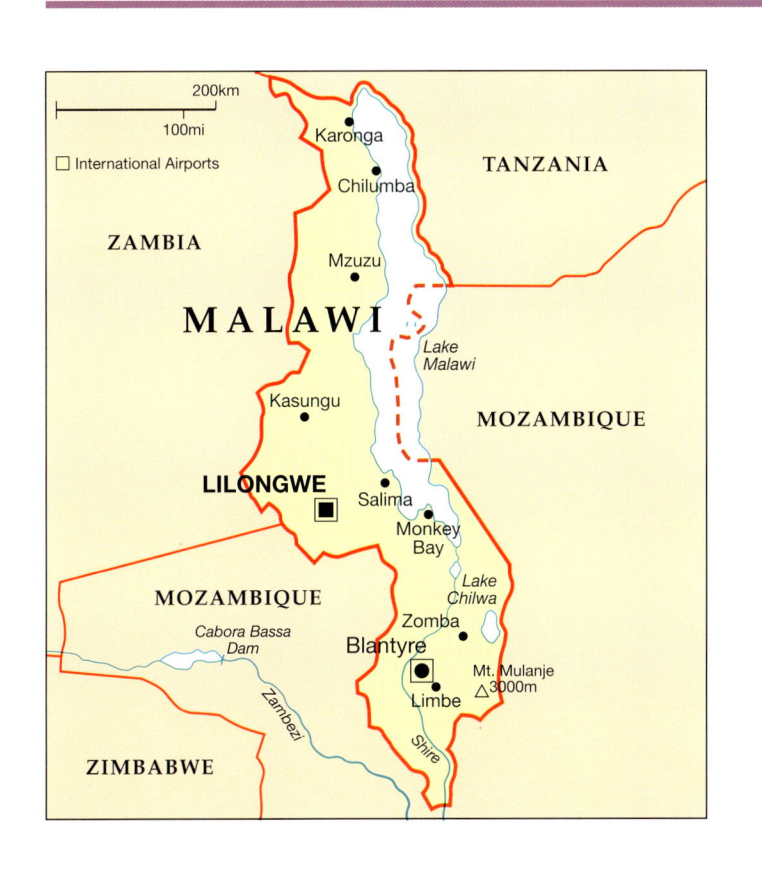

MALAWI

Facts and Figures

Capital: Lilongwe 275,000 (1992)
Area (sq km): 118,480
Population: 9,700,000 (1991)
Language: Chichewe, English
Religion: Protestant 64% RC 17% Muslim 12%
Currency: Kwacha = 100 tambala
Annual Income per person: $230
Annual Trade per person: $138
Adult Literacy: 22%
Life Expectancy (F): 50
Life Expectancy (M): 48

59

MALI

Facts and Figures

Capital: Bamako 745,000 (1992)
Area (sq km): 1,240,000
Population: 9,362,000 (1990)
Language: French, Bambara
Religion: Sunni Muslim 90% Traditional 9%
Currency: CFA Franc = 100 centimes
Annual Income per person: $280
Annual Trade per person: $97
Adult Literacy: 33%
Life Expectancy (F): 48
Life Expectancy (M): 40

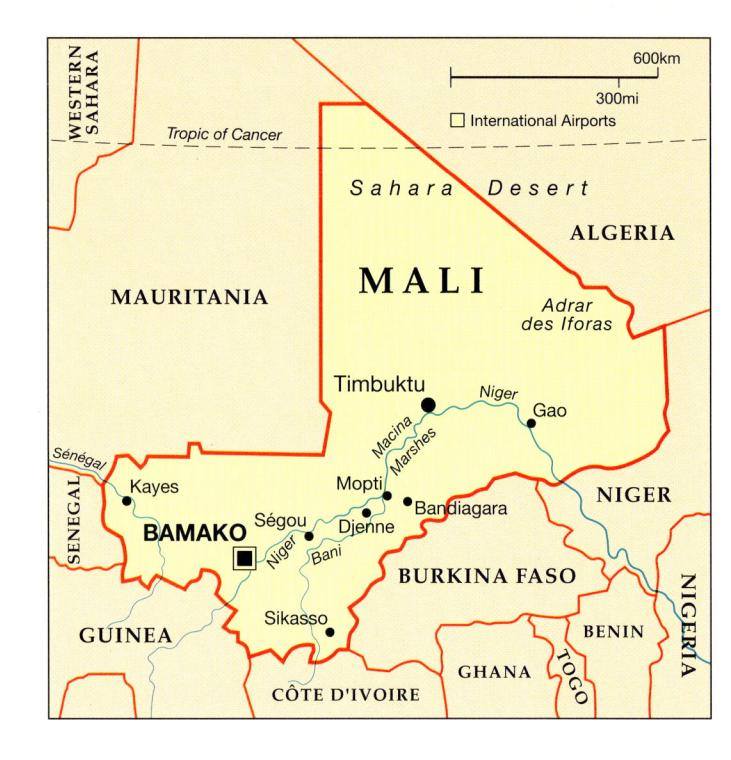

MAURITANIA

Facts and Figures

Capital: Nouakchott 440,600 (1992)
Area (sq km): 1,025,520
Population: 2,110,000 (1992)
Language: Arabic, French, Pulaar, Soninke, Wolof
Religion: Sunni Muslim 99%
Currency: Ouguiya = 5 khoumi
Annual Income per person: $510
Annual Trade per person: $335
Adult Literacy: 34%
Life Expectancy (F): 50
Life Expectancy (M): 46

MAURITIUS

Facts and Figures

Capital: Port Louis 143,000 (1992)
Area (sq km): 2,040
Population: 1,092,400 (1992)
Language: English, Creole, Hindi, French
Religion: Hindu 49% RC 26% Muslim 16%
Currency: Mauritius Rupee = 100 cents
Annual Income per person: $2,420
Annual Trade per person: $2,586
Adult Literacy: 83%
Life Expectancy (F): 73
Life Expectancy (M): 68

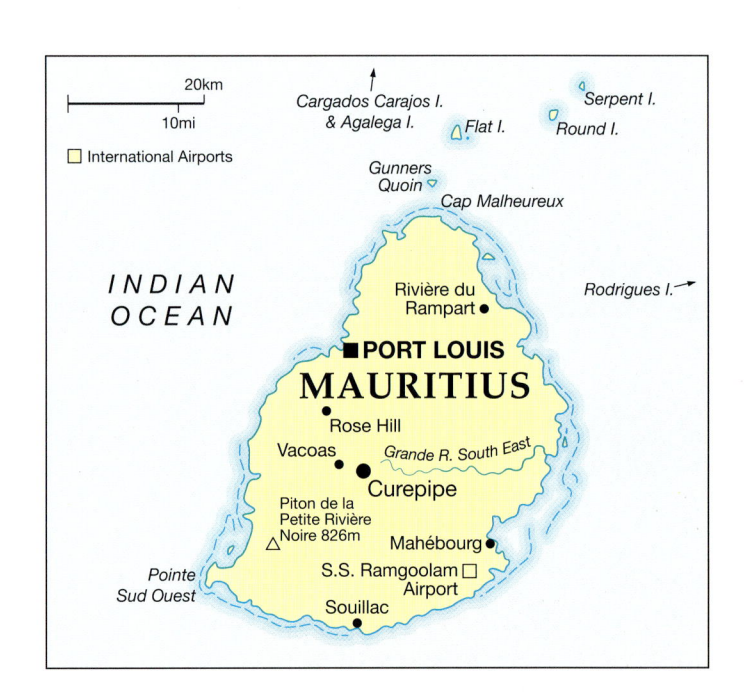

MOROCCO

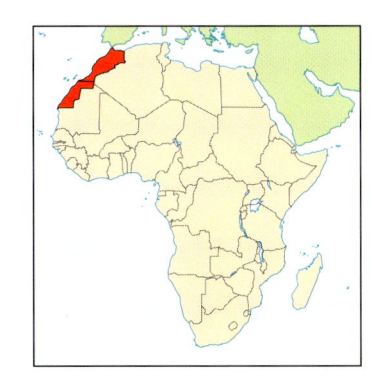

Facts and Figures

Capital: Rabat 650,000 (1982)
Area (sq km): 458,730
Population: 25,700,00 (1991)
Language: Arabic, Berber
Religion: Sunni Muslim 98%
Currency: Dirham = 100 centimes
Annual Income per person: $1,030
Annual Trade per person: $434
Adult Literacy: 50%
Life Expectancy (F): 65
Life Expectancy (M): 62

MOZAMBIQUE

Facts and Figures

Capital: Maputo 1,098,000 (1991)
Area (sq km): 799,380
Population: 16,110,000 (1991)
Language: Portuguese, Bantu
Religion: Traditional 60% RC 18% Muslim 13%
Currency: Metical = 100 centavos
Annual Income per person: $70
Annual Trade per person: $66
Adult Literacy: 35%
Life Expectancy (F): 50
Life Expectancy (M): 47

NAMIBIA

Facts and Figures

Capital: Windhoek 159,000 (1991)
Area (sq km): 824,270
Population: 1,510,000 (1992)
Language: English, Afrikaans, German
Religion: Lutheran 51%
Other Christian 49% Animist
Currency: Namibia $ & S. African Rand
Annual Income per person: $1,120
Annual Trade per person: $1,200
Adult Literacy: 38%
Life Expectancy (F): 60
Life Expectancy (M): 58

NIGER

Facts and Figures

Capital: Niamey 450,000 (1992)
Area (sq km): 1,267,000
Population: 8,040,000 (1991)
Language: French, Hausa
Religion: Sunni Muslim 71%
Christian Traditional
Currency: CFA Franc = 100 centimes
Annual Income per person: $300
Annual Trade per person: $87
Adult Literacy: 29%
Life Expectancy (F): 48
Life Expectancy (M): 45

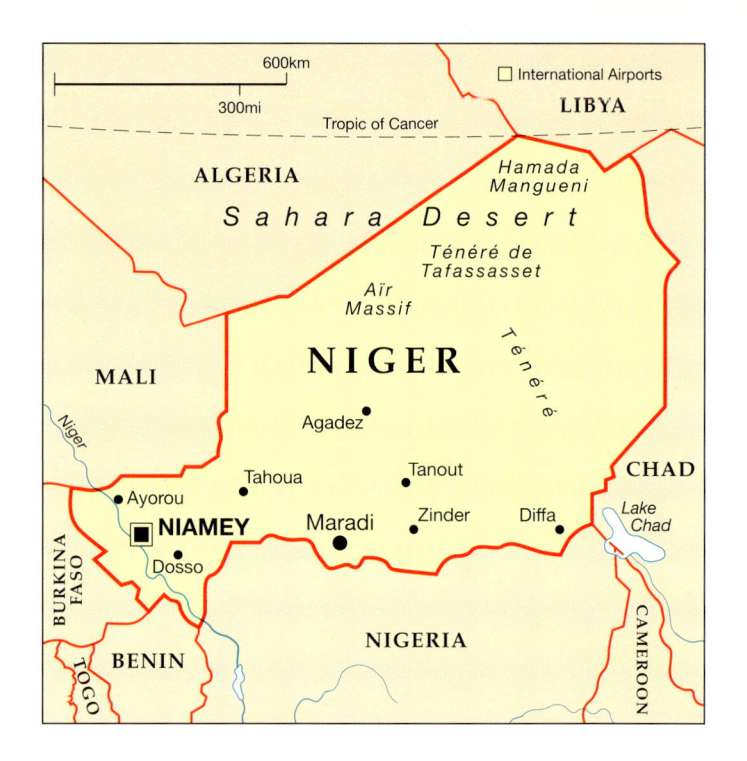

NIGERIA

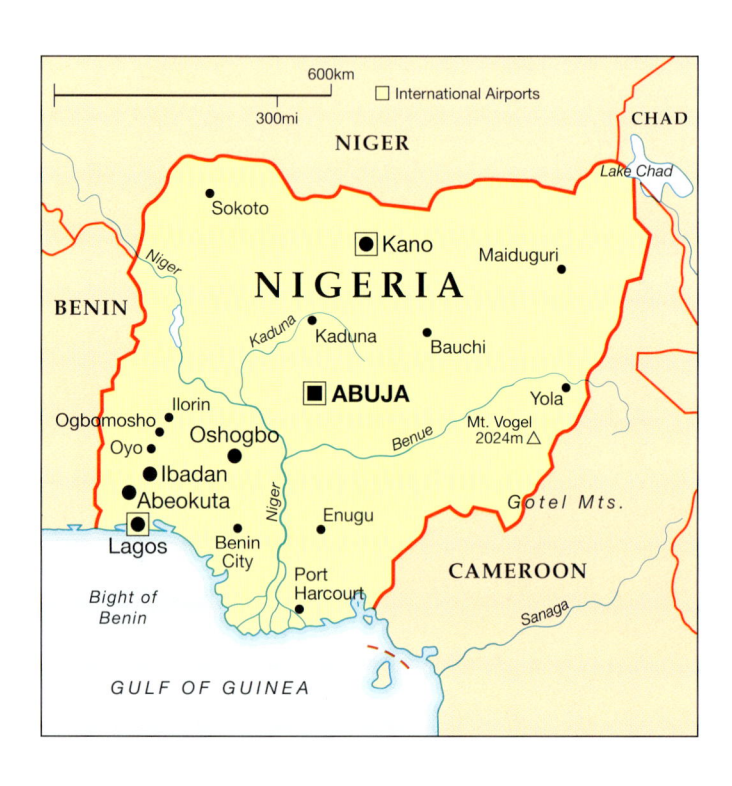

Facts and Figures

Capital: Abuja 305,900 (1992)
Area (sq km): 923,770
Population: 92,800,000 (1991)
Language: English, Hausa, Ibo, Yoruba
Religion: Muslim 48% Protestant 17%
RC 17% Traditional
Currency: Naira = 100 kobo
Annual Income per person: $290
Annual Trade per person: $159
Adult Literacy: 51%
Life Expectancy (F): 54
Life Expectancy (M): 51

RWANDA

Facts and Figures

Capital: Kigali 156,650 (1981)
Area (sq km): 26,340
Population: 7,430,000 (1991)
Language: Kinyarwanda, French,
Kiswahili, Watusi
Religion: Roman Catholic 61%
Protestant 9%
Muslim 9% Traditional
Currency: Rwanda Franc = 100 centimes
Annual Income per person: $260
Annual Trade per person: $70
Adult Literacy: 50%
Life Expectancy (F): 52
Life Expectancy (M): 49

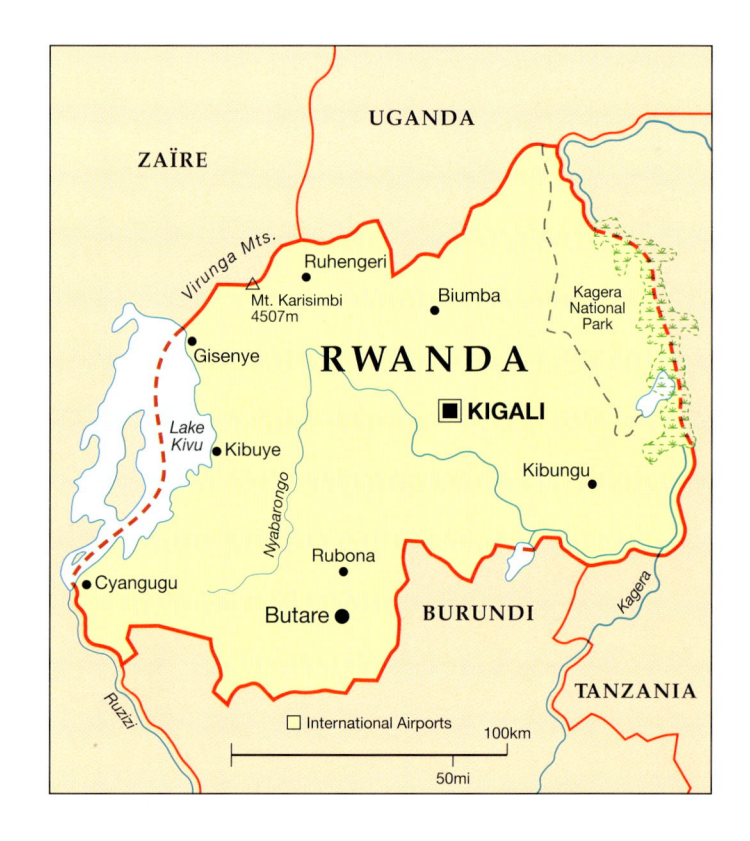

62

SÃO TOMÉ & PRÍNCIPE

Facts and Figures

Capital: São Tomé 35,000 (1984)
Area (sq km): 1,001
Population: 124,000 (1991)
Language: Portugese, Fang
Religion: Roman Catholic 80%
Currency: Dobra = 100 centimos
Annual Income per person: $350
Annual Trade per person: $200
Adult Literacy: 63%
Life Expectancy (F): 68
Life Expectancy (M): 64

SENEGAL

Facts and Figures

Capital: Dakar 1,730,000 (1992)
Area (sq km): 197,160
Population: 7,970,000 (1993)
Language: French, Wolof
Religion: Sunni Muslim 91% Christian Animist
Currency: CFA Franc = 100 centimes
Annual Income per person: $720
Annual Trade per person: $235
Adult Literacy: 38%
Life Expectancy (F): 50
Life Expectancy (M): 48

SEYCHELLES

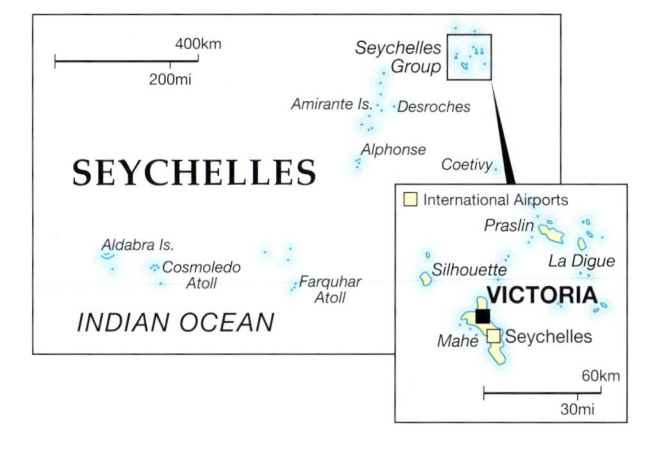

Facts and Figures

Capital: Victoria 24,000 (1992)
Area (sq km): 455
Population: 80,000 (1991)
Language: English, French, Creole
Religion: Roman Catholic 92%
Currency: Seychelles Rupee = 100 cents
Annual Income per person: $5,110
Annual Trade per person: $3,157
Adult Literacy: 89%
Life Expectancy (F): 75
Life Expectancy (M): 65

SIERRA LEONE

Facts and Figures

Capital: Freetown 550,000 (1992)
Area (sq km): 73,330
Population: 4,260,000 (1991)
Language: English, Creole
Religion: Traditional 52% Muslim 39% Christian
Currency: Leone = 100 cents
Annual Income per person: $210
Annual Trade per person: $72
Adult Literacy: 21%
Life Expectancy (F): 45
Life Expectancy (M): 41

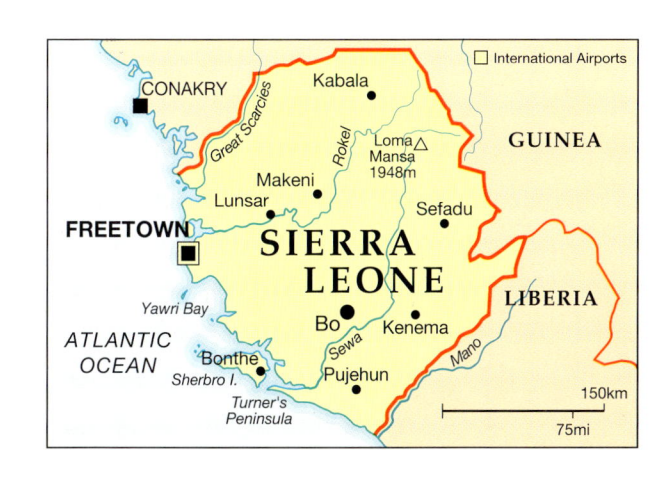

SOMALIA

Facts and Figures

Capital: Mogadishu 485,000 (1992)
Area (sq km): 637,660
Population: 8,000,000 (1990)
Language: Somali, Arabic, English, Italian
Religion: Sunni Muslim 99%
Currency: Somali Shilling = 100 cents
Annual Income per person: $150
Annual Trade per person: $35
Adult Literacy: 25%
Life Expectancy (F): 49
Life Expectancy (M): 45

SOUTH AFRICA

Facts and Figures

Capital: Pretoria 525,600 (1991)
Area (sq km): 1,126,771
Population: 42,500,000 (1993)
Language: Afrikaans, English, Xhosa, Zulu
Religion: Black Christian 42%
Dutch Reform 23%
Roman Catholic 15%
Currency: Rand = 100 cents
Annual Income per person: $2,600
Annual Trade per person: $964
Adult Literacy: 70%
Life Expectancy (F): 66
Life Expectancy (M): 60

SUDAN

Facts and Figures

Capital: Khartoum 625,000 (1992)
Area (sq km): 2,505,810
Population: 30,830,000 (1993)
Language: Arabic, Nubian, English
Religion: Sunni Muslim 71%
Traditional 16% Christian 8%
Currency: Dinar = 100 piastres
Annual Income per person: $450
Annual Trade per person: $66
Adult Literacy: 27%
Life Expectancy (F): 53
Life Expectancy (M): 51

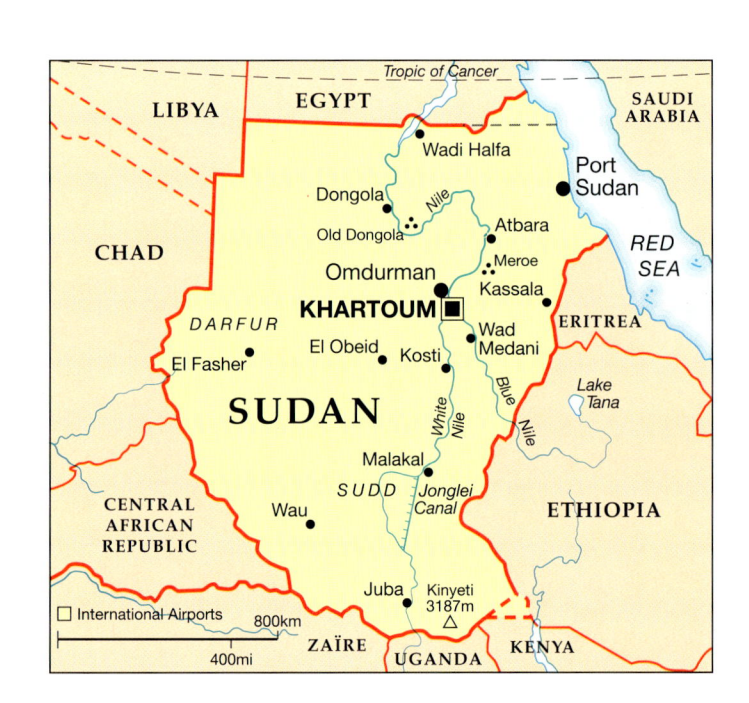

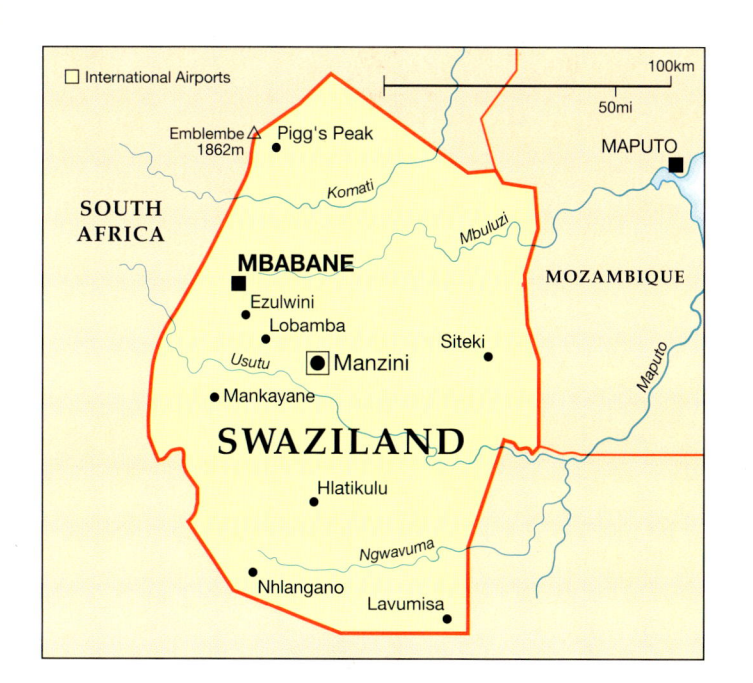

SWAZILAND

Facts and Figures

Capital: Mbabane 45,000 (1992)
Area (sq km): 17,360
Population: 835,000 (1989)
Language: Swazi, English
Religion: Christian 60% Traditional 40%
Currency: Lilangeni = 100 cents
Annual Income per person: $1,060
Annual Trade per person: $1,300
Adult Literacy: 72%
Life Expectancy (F): 60
Life Expectancy (M): 56

TANZANIA

Facts and Figures

Capital: Dodoma 225,000 (1992)
Area (sq km): 945,090
Population: 28,200,000 (1991)
Language: Swahili, English
Religion: Christian 40% Muslim 33% Traditional 23%
Currency: Tanzanian Shilling = 100 cents
Annual Income per person: $100
Annual Trade per person: $56
Adult Literacy: 65%
Life Expectancy (F): 55
Life Expectancy (M): 50

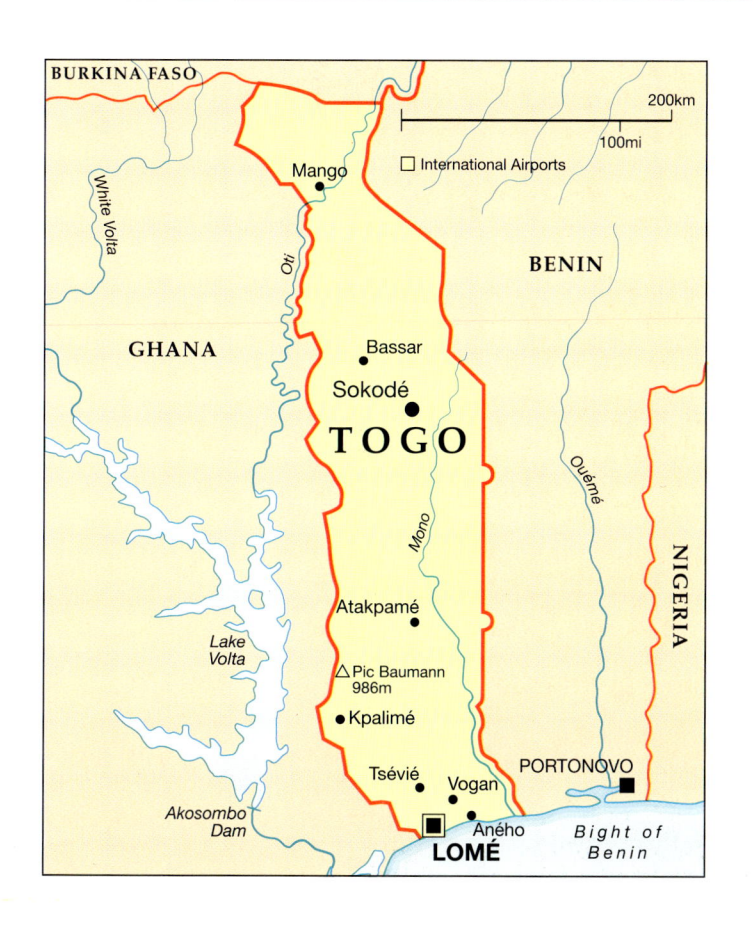

TOGO

Facts and Figures

Capital: Lomé 500,000 (1987)
Area (sq km): 56,790
Population: 4,100,000 (1991)
Language: French, Ewe, Kabiye
Religion: Traditional 50%
Roman Catholic 26%
Muslim 15% Protestant 9%
Currency: CFA Franc = 100 centimes
Annual Income per person: $400
Annual Trade per person: $210
Adult Literacy: 43%
Life Expectancy (F): 57
Life Expectancy (M): 53

65

TUNISIA

Facts and Figures

Capital: Tunis 687,000 (1992)
Area (sq km): 164,150
Population: 8,370,000 (1992)
Language: Arabic, French
Religion: Muslim 97%
Currency: Tunisian Dinar = 1000 millimes
Annual Income per person: $1,510
Annual Trade per person: $1,065
Adult Literacy: 65%
Life Expectancy (F): 69
Life Expectancy (M): 67

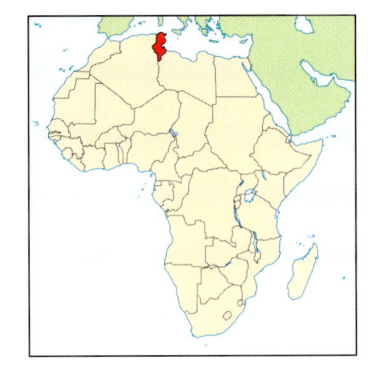

UGANDA

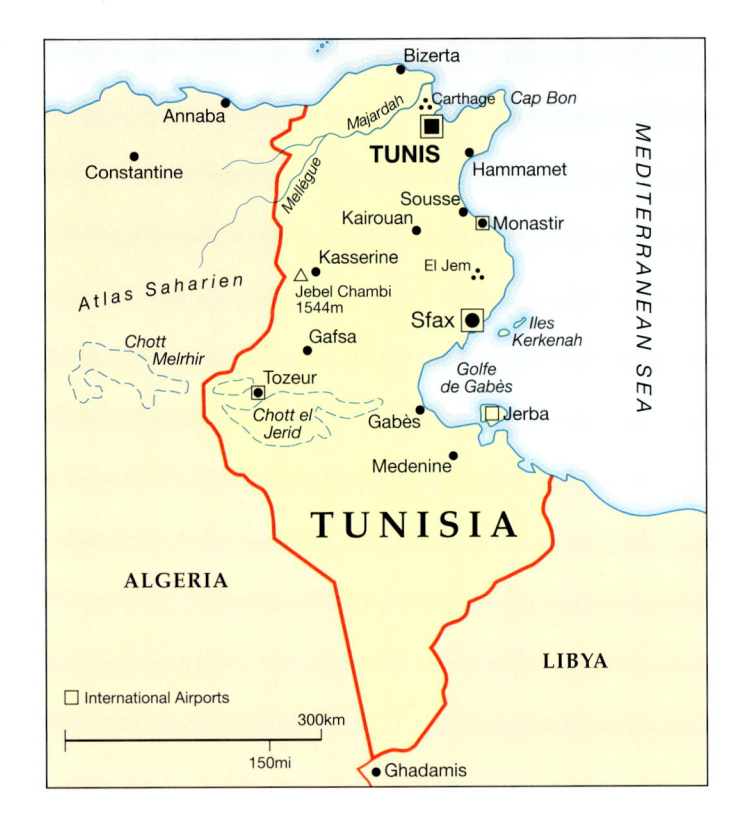

Facts and Figures

Capital: Kampala 773,500 (1991)
Area (sq km): 241,040
Population: 19,600,000 (1991)
Language: English, Swahili, Bantu languages
Religion: Roman Catholic 40%
Protestant 29%
Traditional 18% Muslim 7%
Currency: Uganda Shilling = 100 cents
Annual Income per person: $170
Annual Trade per person: $20
Adult Literacy: 48%
Life Expectancy (F): 55
Life Expectancy (M): 51

ZAIRE

Facts and Figures

Capital: Kinshasa 3,330,000 (1992)
Area (sq km): 2,344,890
Population: 40,256,000 (1991)
Language: French, Swahili, Tshiluba, Kikongo, Lingala
Religion: Roman Catholic 47%
Protestant 28%
Kimbanguiste 17%
Currency: Zaïre = 100 makuta
Annual Income per person: $220
Annual Trade per person: $42
Adult Literacy: 72%
Life Expectancy (F): 56
Life Expectancy (M): 52

ZAMBIA

Facts and Figures

Capital: Lusaka 950,000 (1992)
Area (sq km): 752,610
Population: 8,780,000 (1991)
Language: English, Bantu languages
Religion: Christian 67% Traditional
Currency: Kwacha = 100 negwee
Annual Income per person: $420
Annual Trade per person: $265
Adult Literacy: 73%
Life Expectancy (F): 57
Life Expectancy (M): 54

ZIMBABWE

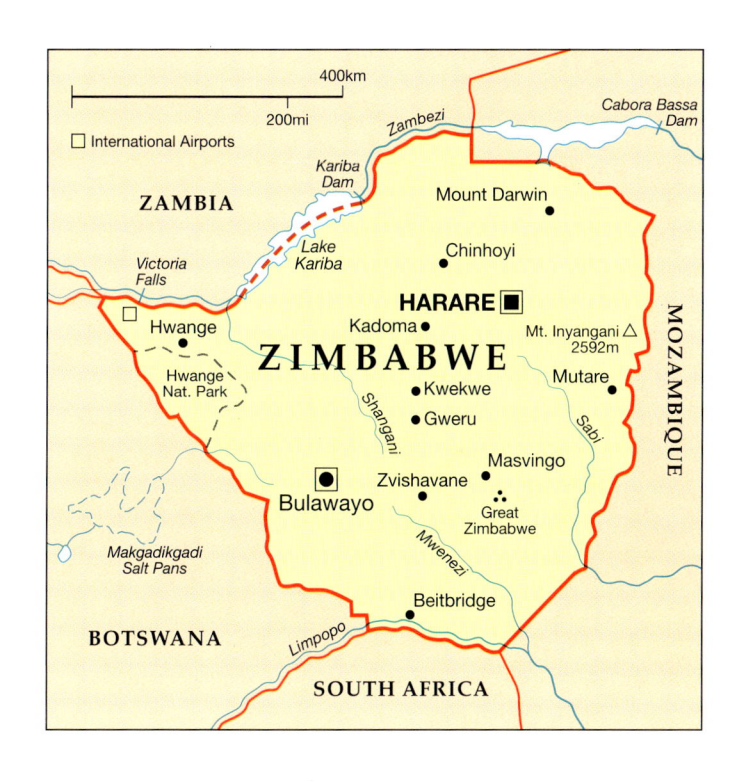

Facts and Figures

Capital: Harare 850,000 (1992)
Area (sq km): 390,000
Population: 10,700,000 (1992)
Language: English, Shona, Ndebele
Religion: Christian 53% Traditional
Currency: Zimbabwe Dollar = 100 cents
Annual Income per person: $620
Annual Trade per person: $381
Adult Literacy: 67%
Life Expectancy (F): 63
Life Expectancy (M): 59

Asia

Asia

COUNTRY	PAGE
Afghanistan	70
Armenia	70
Azerbaijan	70
Bahrain	71
Bangladesh	71
Bhutan	71
Brunei	72
Cambodia	72
China	73
Georgia	72
Hong Kong	73
India	74
Indonesia	74
Iran	74
Iraq	75
Israel	75
Japan	75
Jordan	76
North Korea	76
South Korea	76
Kazakhstan	77
Kuwait	77
Kyrgyzstan	77
Laos	78
Lebanon	78
Malaysia	78
Maldives	79
Mongolia	79
Myanmar (Burma)	79
Nepal	80
Oman	80
Pakistan	80
Philippines	81
Qatar	81
Russia	82
Saudi Arabia	82
Singapore	83
Sri Lanka	83
Syria	83
Taiwan	84
Tajikistan	84
Thailand	84
Turkmenistan	84
United Arab Emirates	85
Uzbekistan	85
Vietnam	85
Yemen	85

AFGHANISTAN

Facts and Figures

Capital: Kabul 913,200 (1979)
Area (sq km): 652,090
Population: 16,560,000 (1990)
Language: Pushtu, Dari
Religion: Sunni Muslim 70%
Shiite Muslim 25%
Currency: Afghani = 100 puls
Annual Income per person: $450
Annual Trade per person: $73
Adult Literacy: 30%
Life Expectancy (F): 44
Life Expectancy (M): 43

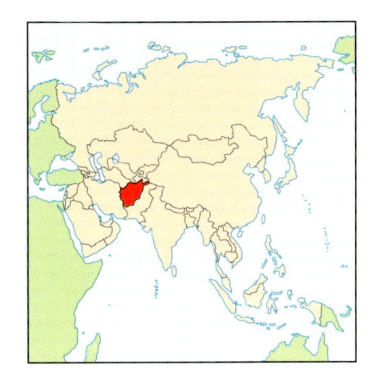

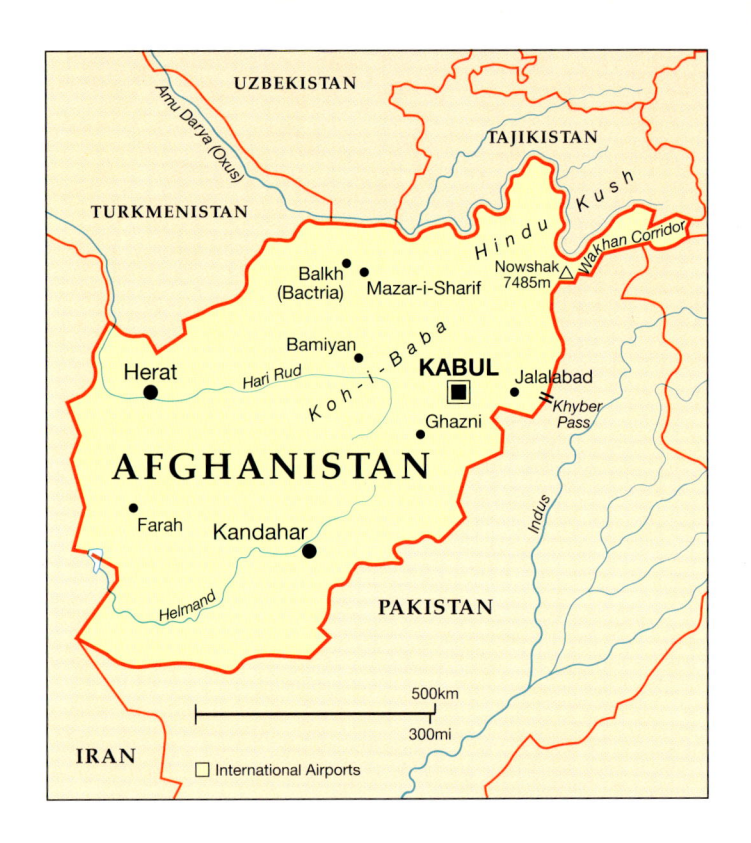

ARMENIA

Facts and Figures

Capital: Yerevan 1,185,000 (1990)
Area (sq km): 29,800
Population: 3,400,000 (1992)
Language: Armenian
Religion: Armenian Orthodox
Currency: Dram
Annual Income per person: $2,150
Annual Trade per person: $500
Adult Literacy: 93%
Life Expectancy (F): 73
Life Expectancy (M): 78

AZERBAIJAN

Facts and Figures

Capital: Baku 1,149,000 (1990)
Area (sq km): 86,600
Population: 7,200,000 (1992)
Language: Azerbaijani
Religion: Shiite Muslim 62%
Sunni Muslim 26%
Currency: Manat
Annual Income per person: $1,670
Annual Trade per person: $400
Adult Literacy: 93%
Life Expectancy (F): 75
Life Expectancy (M): 67

BAHRAIN

Facts and Figures

Capital: Manama 152,000 (1988)
Area (sq km): 688
Population: 538,000 (1993)
Language: Arabic
Religion: Shiite Muslim 60% Sunni Muslim 25% Christian 7%
Currency: Bahrain Dinar = 1000 fils
Annual Income per person: $6,910
Annual Trade per person: $14,094
Adult Literacy: 77%
Life Expectancy (F): 74
Life Expectancy (M): 70

BANGLADESH

Facts and Figures

Capital: Dhaka 3,397,200 (1991)
Area (sq km): 148,400
Population: 118,700,000 (1993)
Language: Bengali, English
Religion: Sunni Muslim 85% Hindu 12%
Currency: Taka = 100 paisa
Annual Income per person: $220
Annual Trade per person: $43
Adult Literacy: 35%
Life Expectancy (F): 53
Life Expectancy (M): 53

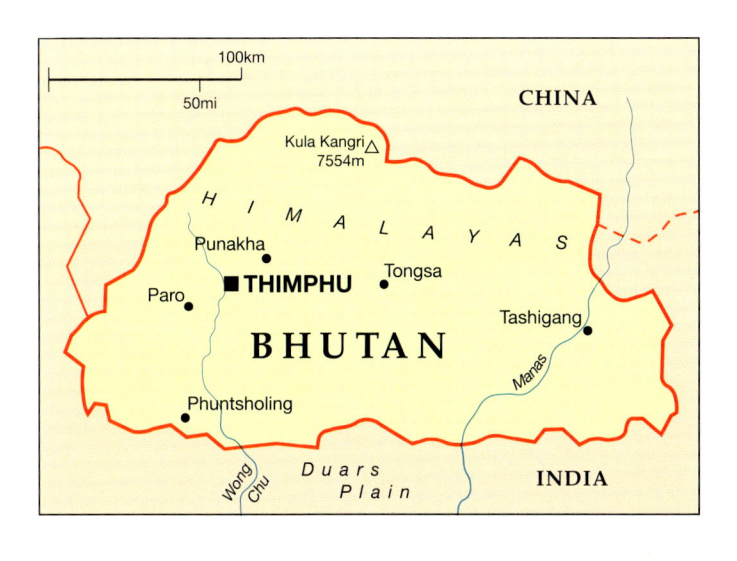

BHUTAN

Facts and Figures

Capital: Thimphu 30,340 (1993)
Area (sq km): 46,500
Population: 600,000 (1990)
Language: Tibetan, Nepalese
Religion: Buddhist 65% Hindu 33%
Currency: Ngultrum = 100 chetrum
Annual Income per person: $468
Annual Trade per person: N/A
Adult Literacy: 35%
Life Expectancy (F): 49
Life Expectancy (M): 51

BRUNEI

Facts and Figures

Capital: Bandar Seri Begawan 45,870 (1991)
Area (sq km): 5,770
Population: 267,800 (1992)
Language: Malay, English, Chinese
Religion: Muslim 67% Buddhist 13% Christian 10%
Currency: Brunei Dollar
Annual Income per person: $15,390
Annual Trade per person: $11,108
Adult Literacy: 86%
Life Expectancy (F): 77
Life Expectancy (M): 74

CAMBODIA

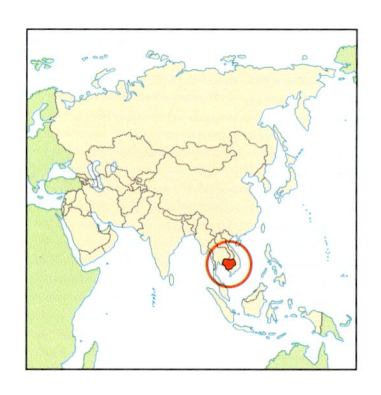

Facts and Figures

Capital: Phnom Penh 800,000 (1989)
Area (sq km): 181,040
Population: 12,000,000 (1993)
Language: Khmer, French
Religion: Buddhist 88%
Currency: Riel = 100 sen
Annual Income per person: $200
Annual Trade per person: $25
Adult Literacy: 35%
Life Expectancy (F): 52
Life Expectancy (M): 50

GEORGIA

Facts and Figures

Capital: Tbilisi 1,283,000 (1991)
Area (sq km): 69,700
Population: 5,460,000 (1990)
Language: Georgian, Armenian, Russian
Religion: Orthodox 83% Muslim 11%
Currency: Rouble = 100 kopeks
Annual Income per person: $1,640
Annual Trade per person: $300
Adult Literacy: Data not available
Life Expectancy (F): 76
Life Expectancy (M): 69

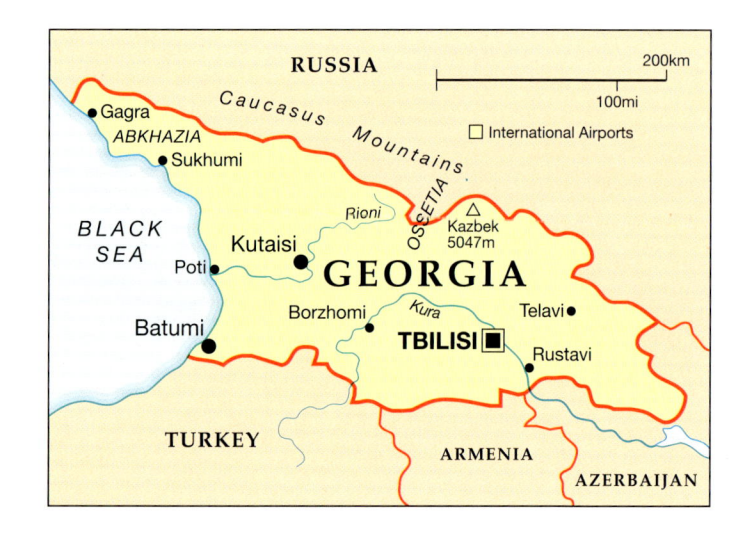

CHINA

Facts and Figures

Capital: Beijing 7,050,000 (1992)
Area (sq km): 9,560,000
Population: 1,158,000,000 (1992)
Language: Chinese
Religion: Confucian 20% Buddhist 6% Taoist 2% Muslim 2%
Currency: Renminbi yuan = 10 jiao = 100 fen
Annual Income per person: $370
Annual Trade per person: $137
Adult Literacy: 70%
Life Expectancy (F): 73
Life Expectancy (M): 69

HONG KONG

Facts and Figures

British Colony until 1997
Area (sq km): 1,040
Population: 5,900,000
Language: English, Chinese
Religion: Buddist, Confucian, Taoist, Christian
Currency: Hong Kong Dollar
Annual Income per person: $13,200
Annual Trade per person: $41,886
Adult Literacy: 90%
Life Expectancy (F): 80
Life Expectancy (M): 75

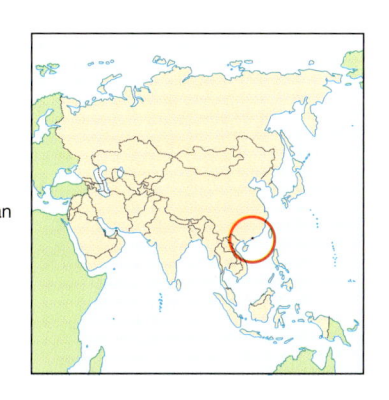

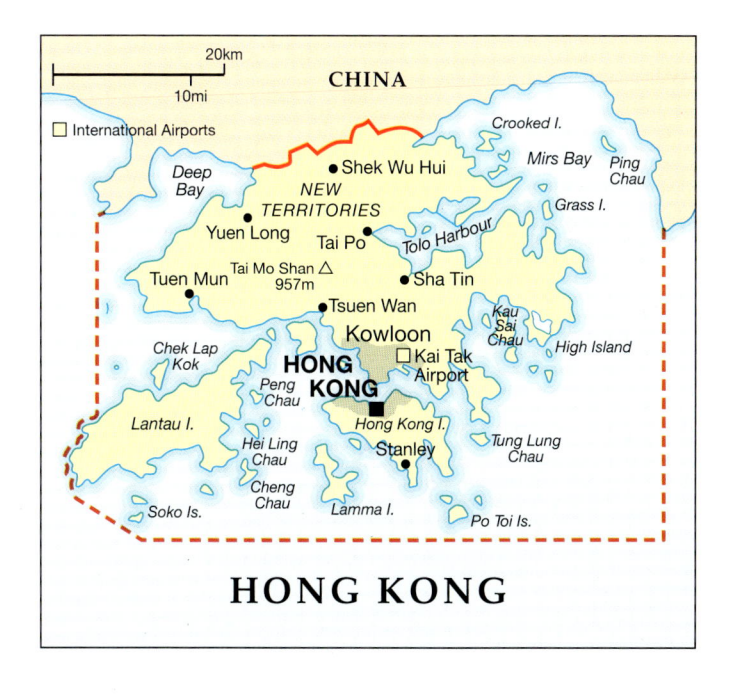

73

INDIA

Facts and Figures

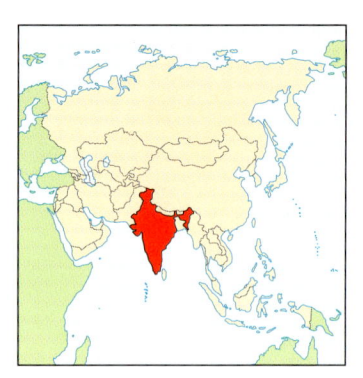

Capital: New Delhi 7,508,000 (1991)
Area (sq km): 3,165,600
Population: 903,000,000 (1991)
Language: Hindi, English, Teluga, Bengali, Marati, Urdu
Religion: Hindu 83% Muslim 11% Christian 2% Sikh 2% Buddhist 1%
Currency: Rupee = 100 paisa
Annual Income per person: $330
Annual Trade per person: $44
Adult Literacy: 48%
Life Expectancy (F): 61
Life Expectancy (M): 60

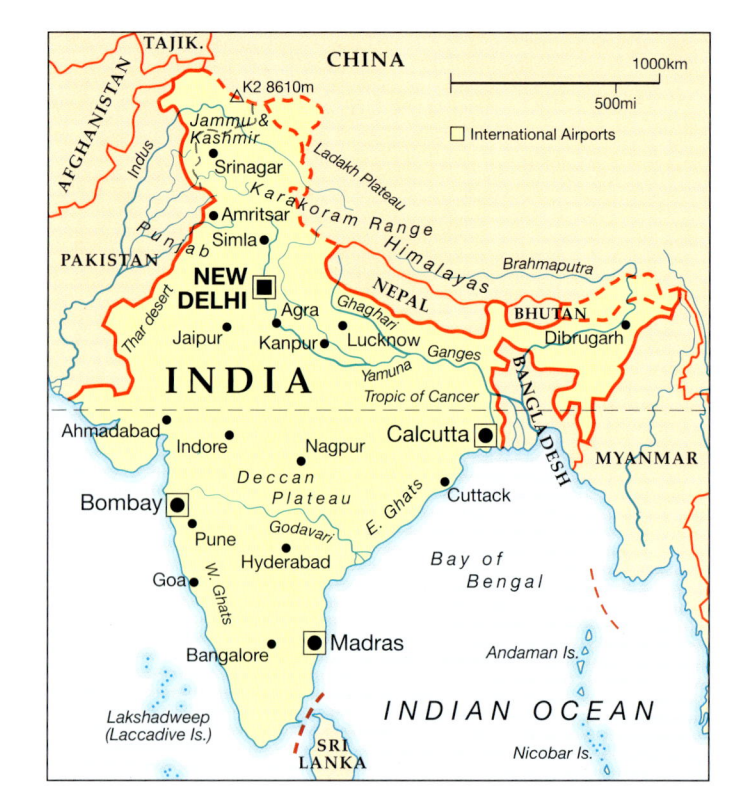

INDONESIA

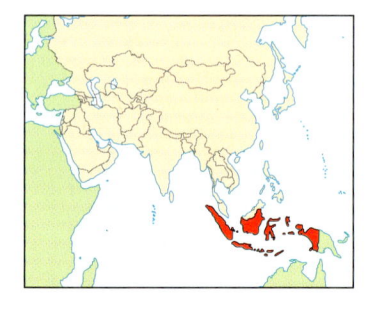

Facts and Figures

Capital: Jakarta 9,000,000 (1993)
Area (sq km): 1,919,440
Population: 187,800,000 (1993)
Language: Bahasa Indonesian, Dutch
Religion: Sunni Muslim 87% Christian 9%
Currency: Rupiah = 100 sen
Annual Income per person: $620
Annual Trade per person: $293
Adult Literacy: 76%
Life Expectancy (F): 65
Life Expectancy (M): 61

IRAN

Facts and Figures

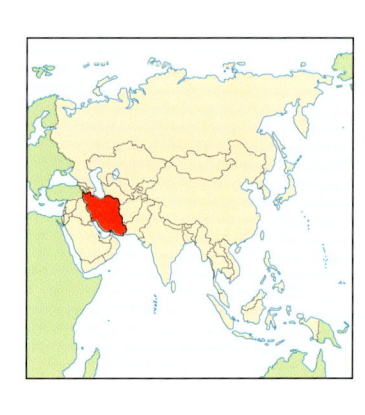

Capital: Tehran 7,214,000 (1992)
Area (sq km): 1,648,000
Population: 61,600,000 (1992)
Language: Farsi, Kurdish, Baluchi
Religion: Shi'ite Muslim 94%
Currency: Rial = 100 dinars
Annual Income per person: $2,320
Annual Trade per person: $598
Adult Literacy: 54%
Life Expectancy (F): 68
Life Expectancy (M): 67

IRAQ

Facts and Figures

Capital: Baghdad 4,914,000 (1992)
Area (sq km): 438,320
Population: 19,410,000 (1993)
Language: Arabic, Kurdish, Turkish
Religion: Shi'ite Muslim 61%
Sunni Muslim 34%
Currency: Dinar = 20 dirhams
Annual Income per person: $2,100
Annual Trade per person: $276
Adult Literacy: 60%
Life Expectancy (F): 67
Life Expectancy (M): 65

ISRAEL

Facts and Figures

Capital: Jerusalem 556,500 (1991)
Area (sq km): 27,010
Population: 7,200,000
Language: Hebrew, Arabic, English
Religion: Jewish 78% Muslim 13%
Christian 2%
Currency: Shekel = 100 agorot
Annual Income per person: $11,330
Annual Trade per person: $5,794
Adult Literacy: 96%
Life Expectancy (F): 78
Life Expectancy (M): 74

JAPAN

Facts and Figures

Capital: Tokyo 7,976,000 (1992)
Area (sq km): 377,750
Population: 124,900,000 (1992)
Language: Japanese, Korean, Chinese
Religion: Shintoism, Buddhism
Currency: Yen = 100 sen
Annual Income per person: $29,794
Annual Trade per person: $4,617
Adult Literacy: 99%
Life Expectancy (F): 82
Life Expectancy (M): 76

JORDAN

Facts and Figures

Capital: Amman 1,272,000 (1992)
Area (sq km): 97,740
Population: 4,010,000 (1992)
Language: Arabic
Religion: Sunni Muslim 95% Christian 5%
Currency: Jordanian Dinar = 1000 fils
Annual Income per person: $1,120
Annual Trade per person: $825
Adult Literacy: 80%
Life Expectancy (F): 70
Life Expectancy (M): 66

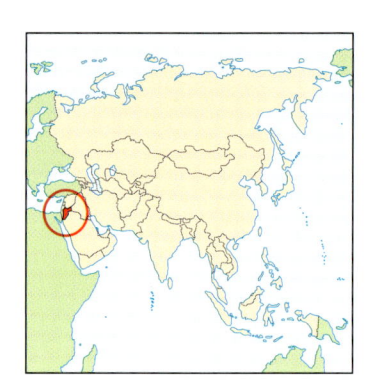

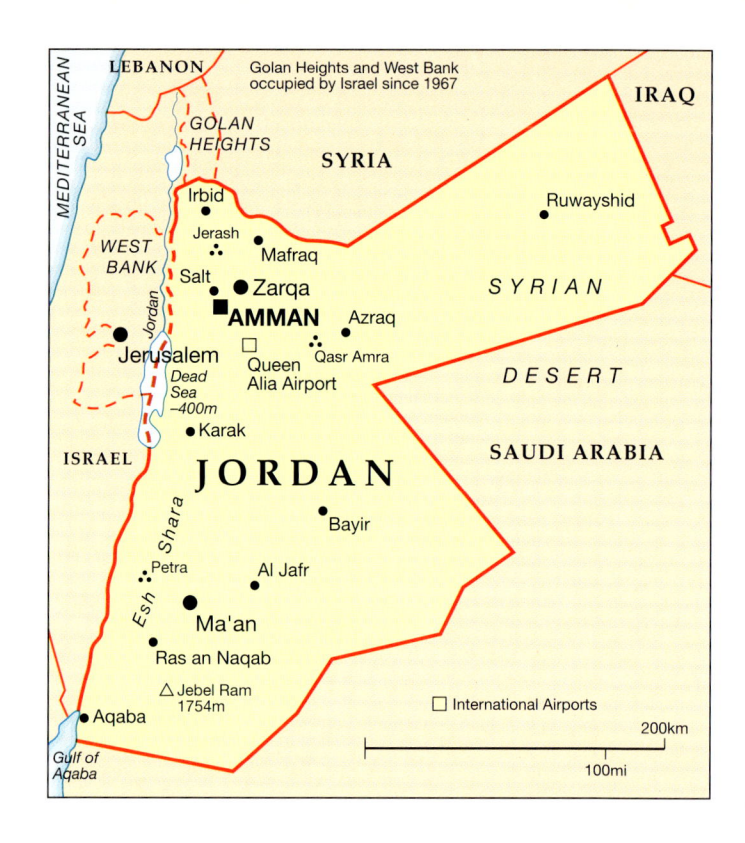

NORTH KOREA

Facts and Figures

Capital: Pyongyang 2,567,000 (1992)
Area (sq km): 122,762
Population: 22,030,000 (1991)
Language: Korean, Chinese
Religion: Chondogyo 14% Traditional 14% Buddhist 2% Christian 1%
Currency: North Korean Won = 100 chon
Annual Income per person: $1,100
Annual Trade per person: $200
Adult Literacy: 99%
Life Expectancy (F): 72
Life Expectancy (M): 66

SOUTH KOREA

Facts and Figures

Capital: Seoul 10,268,000 (1990)
Area (sq km): 99,270
Population: 43,663,000 (1990)
Language: Korean
Religion: Buddhist 24% Protestant 16% RC 5% Confucian 2%
Currency: South Korean Won = 100 chon
Annual Income per person: $6,743
Annual Trade per person: $3,546
Adult Literacy: 96%
Life Expectancy (F): 73
Life Expectancy (M): 67

KAZAKHSTAN

Facts and Figures

Capital: Alma-Ata 1,166,000 (1992)
Area (sq km): 2,717,300
Population: 17,200,000 (1992)
Language: Kazakh, Russian
Religion: Sunni Muslim, Christian
Currency: Tenge = 500 rubles
Annual Income per person: $2,470
Annual Trade per person: $500
Adult Literacy: Data not available
Life Expectancy (F): 73
Life Expectancy (M): 64

KUWAIT

Facts and Figures

Capital: Kuwait City 31,300 (1993)
Area (sq km): 17,820
Population: 2,100,000 (1991)
Language: Arabic, English
Religion: Sunni Muslim 78%
Shiite Muslim 14% Christian 6%
Currency: Kuwaiti Dinar = 1000 fils
Annual Income per person: $16,380
Annual Trade per person: $8,682
Adult Literacy: 74%
Life Expectancy (F): 77
Life Expectancy (M): 72

KYRGYZSTAN

Facts and Figures

Capital: Bishkek 641,400 (1991)
Area (sq km): 198,500
Population: 4,500,000 (1992)
Language: Kirghiz
Religion: Sunni Muslim, Christian
Currency: Som = 100 tiyin
Annual Income per person: $1,550
Annual Trade per person: $30
Adult Literacy: Data not available
Life Expectancy (F): 73
Life Expectancy (M): 65

77

LAOS

Facts and Figures

Capital: Vientiane 454,000 (1992)
Area (sq km): 236,800
Population: 4,400,000 (1993)
Language: Lao, French, English
Religion: Buddhist 52% Traditional 33%
Currency: Kip = 100 cents
Annual Income per person: $230
Annual Trade per person: $62
Adult Literacy: 84%
Life Expectancy (F): 53
Life Expectancy (M): 50

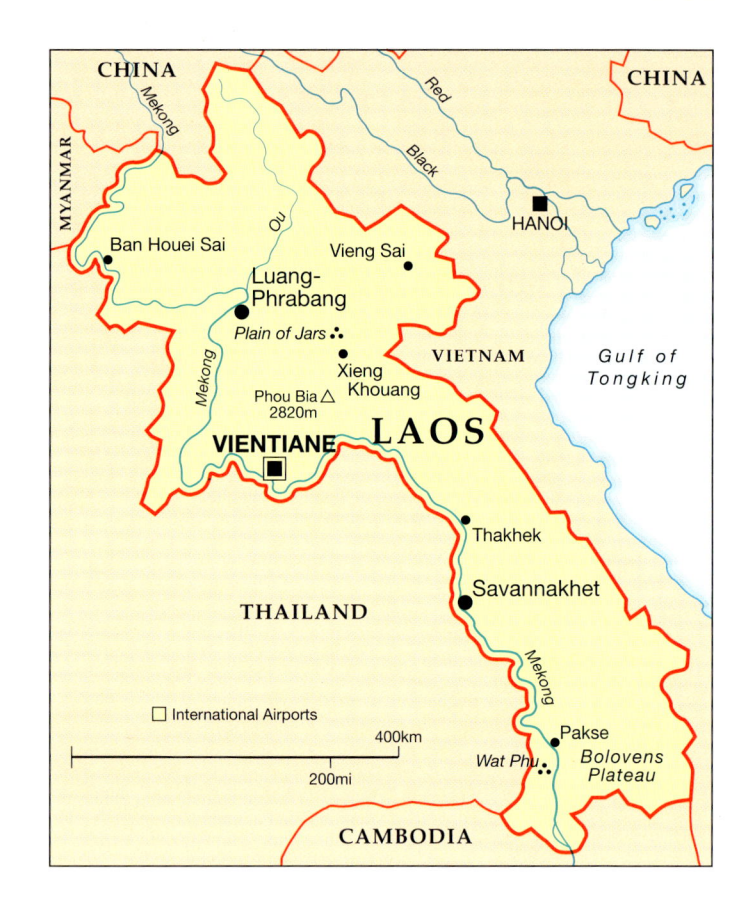

LEBANON

Facts and Figures

Capital: Beirut 1,500,000 (1992)
Area (sq km): 10,400
Population: 2,760,000 (1991)
Language: Arabic, French, English, Armenian
Religion: Shi'ite Muslim 35% Maronite Christian 27% Sunni Muslim 23%
Currency: Lebanese Pound = 100 piastres
Annual Income per person: $2,000
Annual Trade per person: $750
Adult Literacy: 80%
Life Expectancy (F): 69
Life Expectancy (M): 65

MALAYSIA

Facts and Figures

Capital: Kuala Lumpur 1,233,000 (1990)
Area (sq km): 329,760
Population: 19,030,000 (1993)
Language: Bahasa Malaysian, Chinese, Tamil, English
Religion: Sunni Muslim 53% Buddhist 17% Taoist, Hindu, Christian
Currency: Ringgit = 100 sen
Annual Income per person: $3,265
Annual Trade per person: $3,877
Adult Literacy: 79%
Life Expectancy (F): 73
Life Expectancy (M): 69

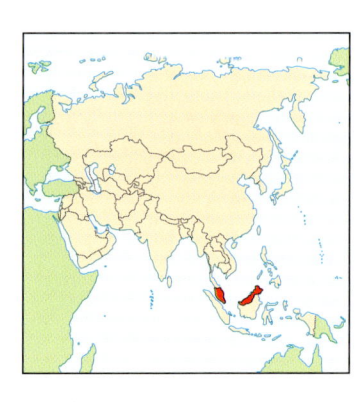

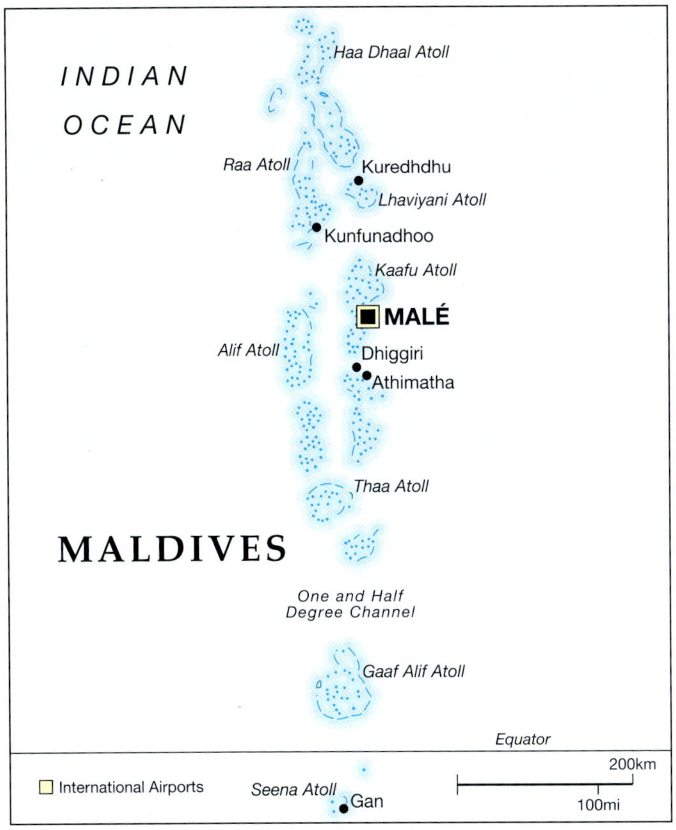

MALDIVES

MALDIVES

Map showing Maldives atolls including Haa Dhaal Atoll, Raa Atoll, Kuredhdhu, Lhaviyani Atoll, Kunfunadhoo, Kaafu Atoll, MALÉ, Alif Atoll, Dhiggiri, Athimatha, Thaa Atoll, One and Half Degree Channel, Gaaf Alif Atoll, Seena Atoll, Gan, Equator, in the Indian Ocean.

Facts and Figures

Capital: Malé 55,130 (1990)
Area (sq km): 298
Population: 238,400 (1993)
Language: Divehi, English, Arabic
Religion: Sunni Muslim
Currency: Rufiyaa = 100 laari
Annual Income per person: $460
Annual Trade per person: $750
Adult Literacy: 92%
Life Expectancy (F): 63
Life Expectancy (M): 61

MYANMAR (BURMA)

Map showing Myanmar with neighboring Bhutan, India, Bangladesh, China, Vietnam, Laos, Thailand; cities Myitkyina, Lashio, Mandalay, Pagan, Mingyan, Sittwe, Pegu, Henzada, YANGON (RANGOON), Moulmein, BANGKOK, Mergui; features Brahmaputra, Ganges, Mekong, Hkakabo Razi 5881m, Tropic of Cancer, Ayeyarwady (Irrawaddy), Salween, Bay of Bengal, Andaman Is. (India), Andaman Sea.

Facts and Figures

Capital: Rangoon 2,458,710 (1983)
Area (sq km): 676,577
Population: 42,330,000 (1993)
Language: Burmese, English
Religion: Buddhist
Currency: Kyat = 100 pyas
Annual Income per person: $500
Annual Trade per person: $24
Adult Literacy: 81%
Life Expectancy (F): 64
Life Expectancy (M): 61

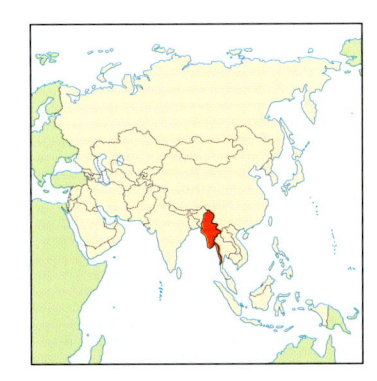

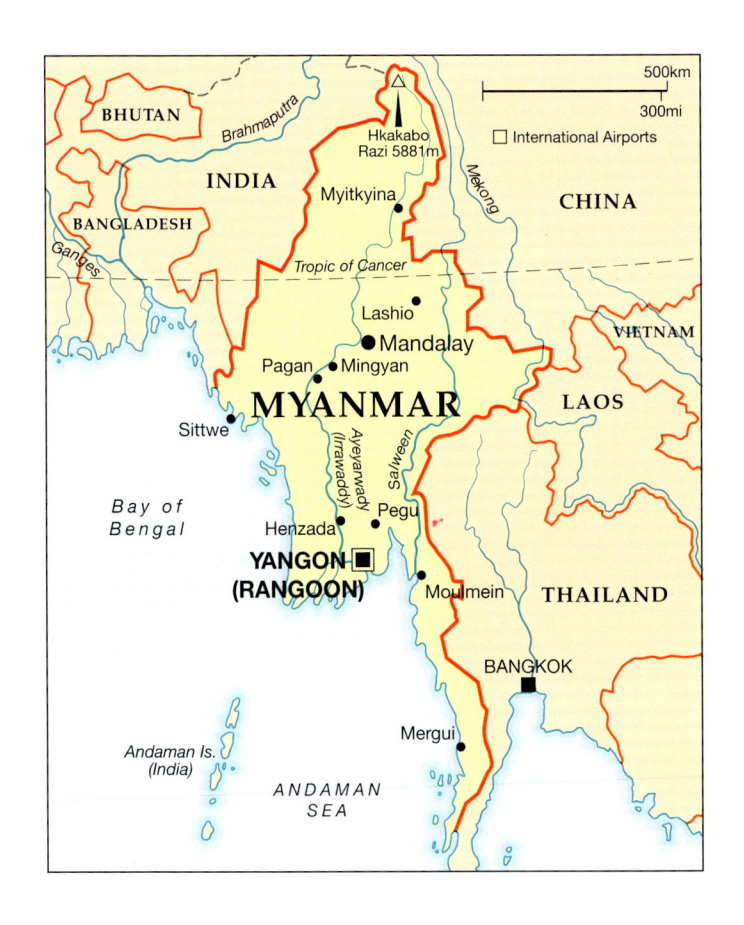

MONGOLIA

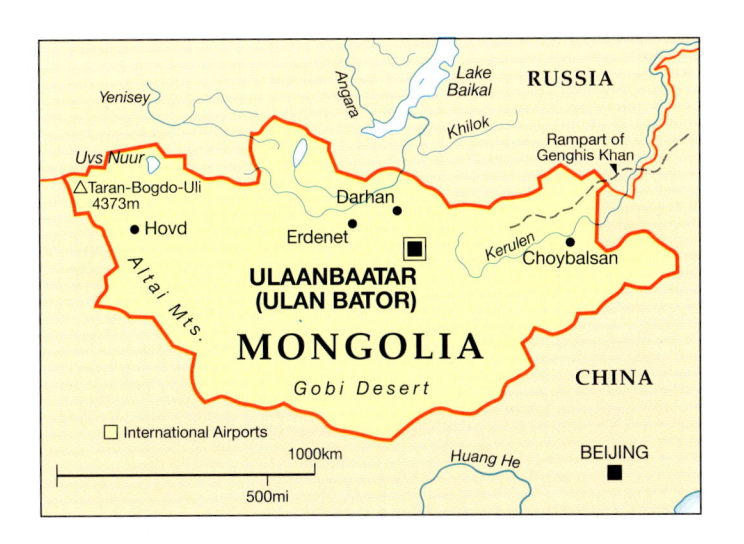

Map showing Mongolia with Russia to the north and China to the south; features Yenisey, Angara, Lake Baikal, Khilok, Rampart of Genghis Khan, Uvs Nuur, Taran-Bogdo-Uli 4373m, Darhan, Hovd, Erdenet, ULAANBAATAR (ULAN BATOR), Kerulen, Choybalsan, Altai Mts., Gobi Desert, Huang He, BEIJING.

Facts and Figures

Capital: Ulan Bator 55,000 (1991)
Area (sq km): 1,566,500
Population: 2,260,000 (1992)
Language: Halh Mongol, Chinese, Russian
Religion: Shamanist 31% Muslim 4% Buddhist
Currency: Tugrik = 100 mongo
Annual Income per person: $600
Annual Trade per person: $400
Adult Literacy: 91%
Life Expectancy (F): 65
Life Expectancy (M): 62

NEPAL

Facts and Figures

Capital: Kathmandu 419,000 (1991)
Area (sq km): 147,200
Population: 19,360,000 (1991)
Language: Nepalese, Tibetan
Religion: Hindu 89% Buddhist 5%
Currency: Nepalese Rupee = 100 paisa
Annual Income per person: $180
Annual Trade per person: $54
Adult Literacy: 26%
Life Expectancy (F): 53
Life Expectancy (M): 54

OMAN

Facts and Figures

Capital: Muscat 320,000 (1992)
Area (sq km): 309,500
Population: 2,070,000 (1991)
Language: Arabic, English, Baluchi
Religion: Muslim 86%
Currency: Omani Rial = 1000 baiza
Annual Income per person: $5,500
Annual Trade per person: $5,172
Adult Literacy: 35%
Life Expectancy (F): 70
Life Expectancy (M): 66

PAKISTAN

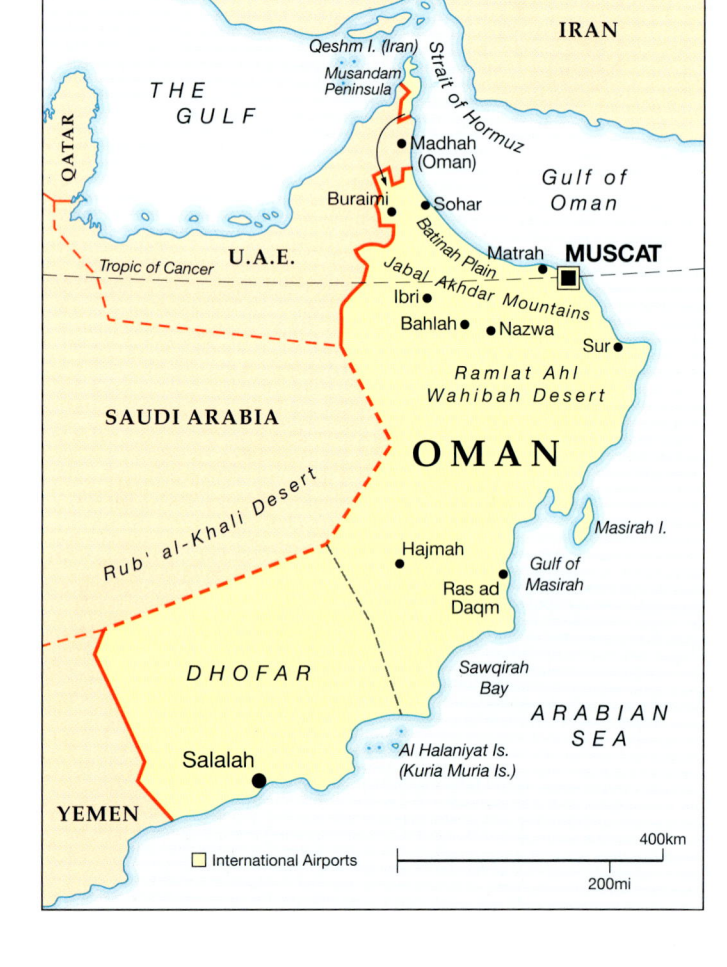

Facts and Figures

Capital: Islamabad 272,000 (1992)
Area (sq km): 796,100
Population: 122,400,000 (1992)
Language: Urdu, Punjabi, Sindhi, Baluchi, Pushtu, English
Religion: Muslim 96% Hindu, Christian
Currency: Pakistan Rupee = 100 paisa
Annual Income per person: $400
Annual Trade per person: $129
Adult Literacy: 35%
Life Expectancy (F): 59
Life Expectancy (M): 59

PHILIPPINES

Facts and Figures

Capital: Manila 1,599,000 (1990)
Area (sq km): 300,000
Population: 65,650,000 (1993)
Language: Pilipino, English
Religion: RC 76% Protestant 5% Sunni Muslim 4%
Currency: Piso = 100 sentimos
Annual Income per person: $740
Annual Trade per person: $332
Adult Literacy: 90%
Life Expectancy (F): 70
Life Expectancy (M): 63

QATAR

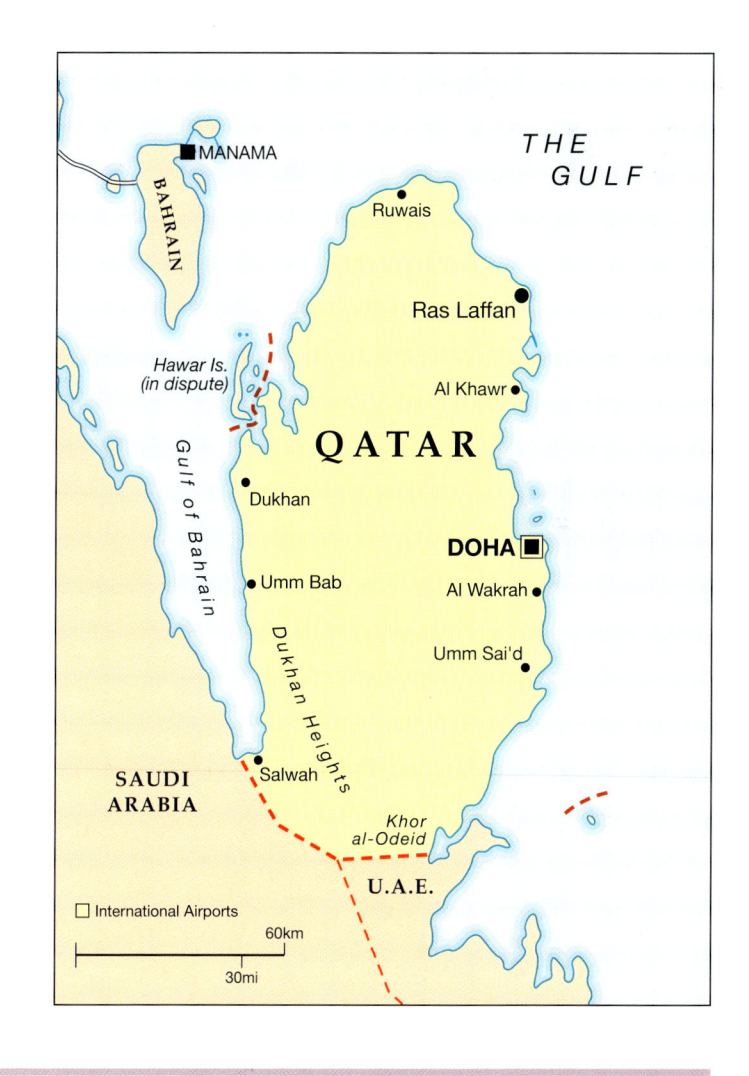

Facts and Figures

Capital: Doha 286,000 (1992)
Area (sq km): 11,500
Population: 510,000
Language: Arabic
Religion: Sunni Muslim 92%
Currency: Qatari Riyal = 100 dirhams
Annual Income per person: $15,870
Annual Trade per person: $28,296
Adult Literacy: 82%
Life Expectancy (F): 73
Life Expectancy (M): 68

RUSSIA

Facts and Figures

Capital: Moscow 8,967,000 (1990)
Area (sq km): 17,075,000
Population: 148,700,000 (1992)
Language: Russian
Religion: Russian Orthodox 25%, Muslim, Buddhist
Currency: Rouble = 100 kopeks
Annual Income per person: $3,222
Annual Trade per person: $680
Adult Literacy: 94%
Life Expectancy (F): 74
Life Expectancy (M): 64

SAUDI ARABIA

Facts and Figures

Capital: Riyadh 2,320,000 (1992)
Area (sq km): 2,200,000
Population: 16,900,000 (1992)
Language: Arabic
Religion: Sunni Muslim 92%, Shi'ite Muslim 8%
Currency: Rial = 100 halalas
Annual Income per person: $7,070
Annual Trade per person: $4,606
Adult Literacy: 62%
Life Expectancy (F): 68
Life Expectancy (M): 64

SINGAPORE

Facts and Figures

Capital: Singapore 2,820,000 (1992)
Area (sq km): 640
Population: 2,820,000 (1992)
Language: Chinese, Malay, Tamil, English
Religion: Buddhist 28% Taoist 13%
Christian 19% Muslim 16%
Hindu 5%
Currency: Singapore Dollar
Annual Income per person: $13,060
Annual Trade per person: $48,275
Adult Literacy: 88%
Life Expectancy (F): 77
Life Expectancy (M): 72

SRI LANKA

Facts and Figures

Capital: Colombo 615,000 (1990)
Area (sq km): 65,610
Population: 17,400,000 (1992)
Language: Sinhala, Tamil, English
Religion: Buddhist 64% Hindu 13%
Muslim 8% Christian 7%
Currency: Sri Lankan Rupee = 100 cents
Annual Income per person: $539
Annual Trade per person: $293
Adult Literacy: 88%
Life Expectancy (F): 74
Life Expectancy (M): 70

SYRIA

Facts and Figures

Capital: Damascus 1,450,000 (1993)
Area (sq km): 185,180
Population: 13,400,000 (1993)
Language: Arabic, Kurdish, Armenian
Religion: Sunni Muslim 90% Christian 9%
Currency: Syrian Pound = 100 piastres
Annual Income per person: $1,100
Annual Trade per person: $502
Adult Literacy: 64%
Life Expectancy (F): 69
Life Expectancy (M): 65

83

TAIWAN

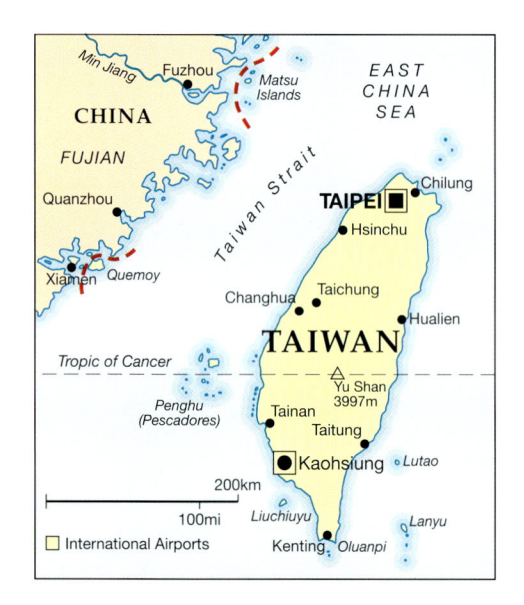

Facts and Figures
Capital: Taipei 2,720,000 (1992)
Area (sq km): 36,100
Population: 20,600,000 (1991)
Language: Mandarin, Chinese
Religion: Buddhist 30% Taoist 18% Christian 4%
Currency: New Taiwan Dollar = 100 cents
Annual Income per person: $8,815
Annual Trade per person: $7,395
Adult Literacy: 91%
Life Expectancy (F): 77
Life Expectancy (M): 72

TAJIKISTAN

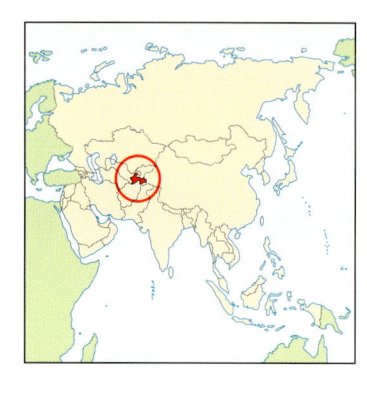

Facts and Figures
Capital: Dushanbe 592,000 (1991)
Area (sq km): 143,100
Population: 5,500,000 (1993)
Language: Tajik, Uzbek, Russian
Religion: Sunni Muslim
Currency: Rouble = 100 kopecks
Annual Income per person: $1,050
Annual Trade per person: $400
Adult Literacy: Data not available
Life Expectancy (F): 72
Life Expectancy (M): 67

TURKMENISTAN

Facts and Figures
Capital: Ashkhabad 411,000 (1990)
Area (sq km): 488,100
Population: 3,800,000 (1992)
Language: Turkmen, Russian
Religion: Muslim 85%
Currency: Manat
Annual Income per person: $1,700
Annual Trade per person: $350
Adult Literacy: Data not available
Life Expectancy (F): 70
Life Expectancy (M): 63

THAILAND

Facts and Figures
Capital: Bangkok 5,876,000 (1990)
Area (sq km): 513,115
Population: 57,800,000 (1993)
Language: Thai, Lao, Chinese, Malay
Religion: Buddhist 94% Muslim 4%
Currency: Baht = 100 satang
Annual Income per person: $1,580
Annual Trade per person: $1,152
Adult Literacy: 93%
Life Expectancy (F): 69
Life Expectancy (M): 65

UZBEKISTAN

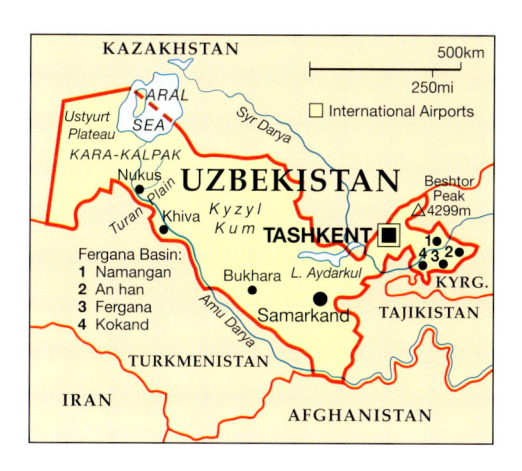

Facts and Figures

Capital: Tashkent 2,115,000 (1991)
Area (sq km): 447,400
Population: 21,200,000 (1992)
Language: Uzbek, Russian, Tajik
Religion: Sunni Muslim 75%
Currency: Rouble = 100 kopeks
Annual Income per person: $1,350
Annual Trade per person: $250
Adult Literacy: 93%
Life Expectancy (F): 73
Life Expectancy (M): 66

UNITED ARAB EMIRATES

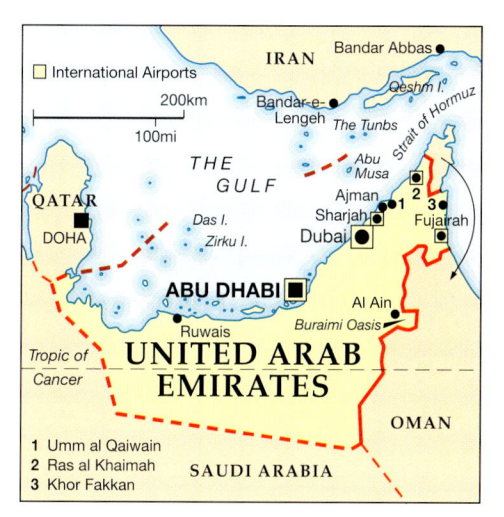

Facts and Figures

Capital: Abu Dhabi 806,000 (1992)
Area (sq km): 83,657
Population: 2,100,000 (1993)
Language: Arabic, English
Religion: Sunni Muslim 96%
Currency: Dirham = 100 fils
Annual Income per person: $19,870
Annual Trade per person: $19,745
Adult Literacy: 55%
Life Expectancy (F): 74
Life Expectancy (M): 70

VIETNAM

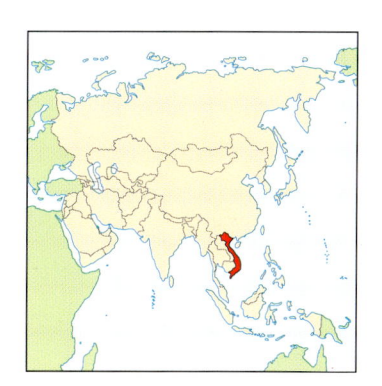

Facts and Figures

Capital: Hanoi 2,100,000 (1992)
Area (sq km): 329,570
Population: 69,300,000 (1992)
Language: Vietnamese
Religion: Buddhist 52% RC 7% Taoist
Currency: Dong = 10 hao
Annual Income per person: $300
Annual Trade per person: $60
Adult Literacy: 88%
Life Expectancy (F): 66
Life Expectancy (M): 62

YEMEN

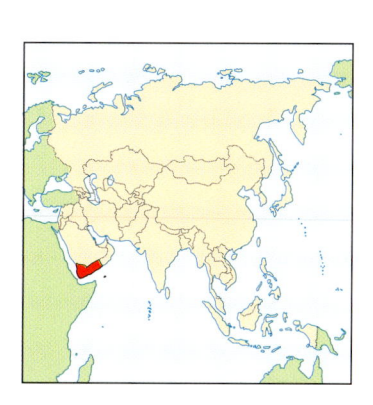

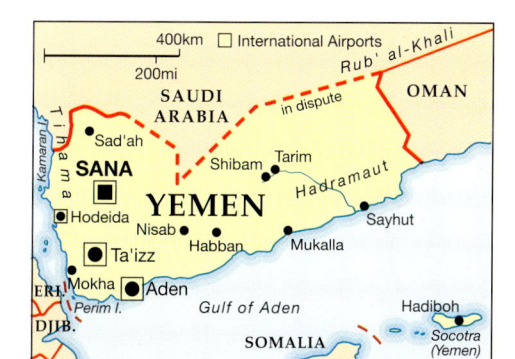

Facts and Figures

Capital: Sana 500,000 (1990)
Area (sq km): 531,000
Population: 13,000,000 (1993)
Language: Arabic
Religion: Sunni Muslim 45%
Shi'ite Muslim 41%
Currency: N. Yemeni Riyal and S. Yemeni Dinar
Annual Income per person: $540
Annual Trade per person: $141
Adult Literacy: 39%
Life Expectancy (F): 52
Life Expectancy (M): 52

Oceania

OCEANIA

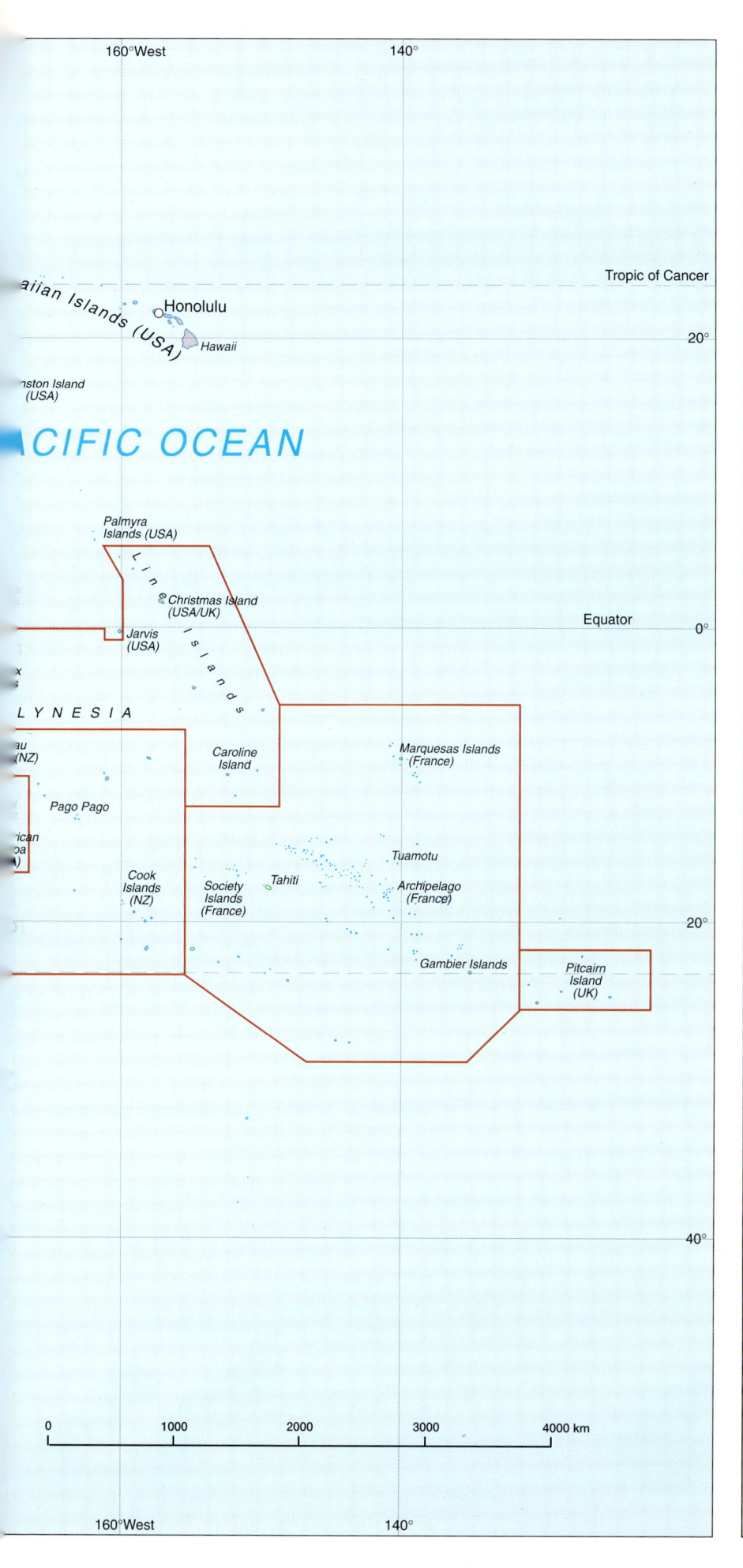

COUNTRY	PAGE
Australia	88
Fiji	88
Kiribati	88
New Zealand	89
Northern Marianas	89
Nauru	89
Marshall Islands	89
Papua New Guinea	90
Palau	90
Solomon Islands	90
Tonga	91
Tuvalu	88
Vanuatu	91
Western Samoa	91

AUSTRALIA

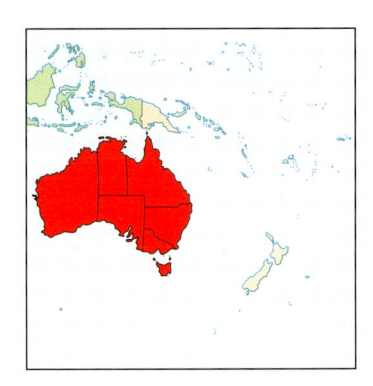

Facts and Figures

Capital: Canberra 278,000 (1991)
Area (sq km): 7,682,300
Population: 17,500,000 (1992)
Language: English
Religion: Catholic 26% Anglican 24% Other Christian 16%
Currency: Australian Dollar
Annual Income per person: $16,590
Annual Trade per person: $4,741
Adult Literacy: 99%
Life Expectancy (F): 80
Life Expectancy (M): 74

FIJI

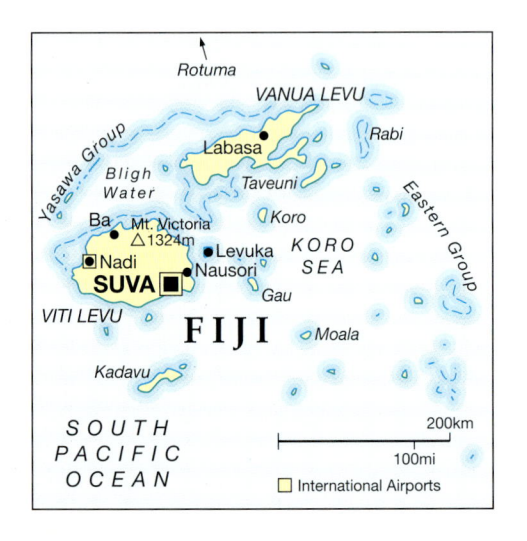

Facts and Figures

Capital: Suva 73,500 (1992)
Area (sq km): 18,333
Population: 758,275 (1993)
Language: English, Bauan, Hindustani
Religion: Christian 50% Hindu 36% Muslim 7%
Currency: Fiji dollar = 100 cents
Annual Income per person: $1,830
Annual Trade per person: $1,491
Adult Literacy: 87%
Life Expectancy (F): 68
Life Expectancy (M): 64

KIRIBATI & TUVALU

Facts and Figures

KIRIBATI

Capital: Bairiki (Tarawa) 25,200
Area (sq km): 720
Population: 72,300 (1991)
Language: English, Gilbertese
Religion: Roman Catholic 53% Protestant 39%
Currency: Australian Dollar
Annual Income per person: $750
Annual Trade per person: $350
Adult Literacy: Data not available
Life Expectancy (F): 58
Life Expectancy (M): 52

Facts and Figures

TUVALU

Capital: Funafuti 3,100 (1992)
Area (sq km): 24
Population: 10,090 (1991)
Language: Tuvaluan, English
Religion: Christian
Currency: Australian Dollar
Annual Income per person: $550
Annual Trade per person: $400
Adult Literacy: 95%
Life Expectancy (F): 63
Life Expectancy (M): 61

MARSHALL ISLANDS

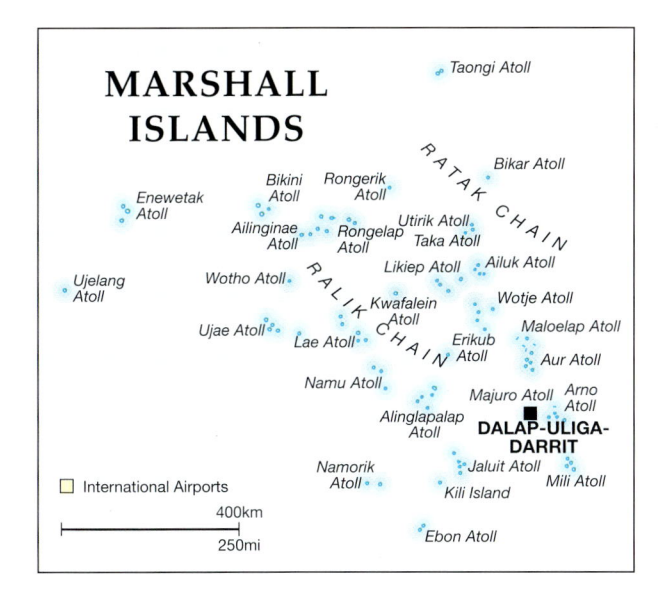

Facts and Figures

Capital: Dalap-Uliga-Darrit 20,000 (1990)
Area (sq km): 181
Population: 45,600 (1990)
Language: Marshallese, English
Religion: Protestant
Currency: US Dollar
Annual Income per person: $1,500
Annual Trade per person: $700
Adult Literacy: 93%
Life Expectancy (F): 64
Life Expectancy (M): 61

NAURU

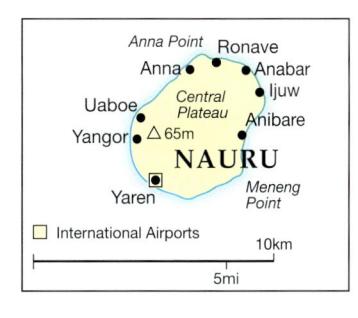

Facts and Figures

Capital: Yaren 7,500 (1990)
Area (sq km): 21
Population: 8,100 (1990)
Language: English, Nauruan
Religion: Roman Catholic, Protestant
Currency: Australian Dollar
Annual Income per person: 10,000
Annual Trade per person: $18,000
Adult Literacy: Data not available
Life Expectancy (F): 69
Life Expectancy (M): 64

NEW ZEALAND

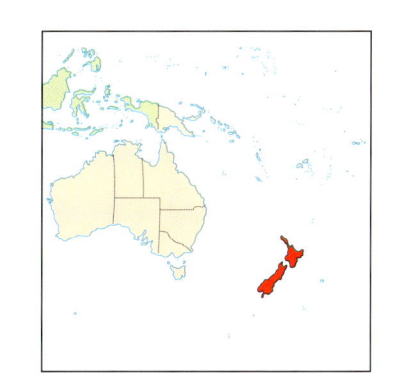

Facts and Figures

Capital: Wellington 325,700 (1992)
Area (sq km): 270,530
Population: 3,495,000 (1993)
Language: English, Maori
Religion: Protestant 44% Roman Catholic 14% Other 7%
Currency: New Zealand Dollar
Annual Income per person: $12,140
Annual Trade per person: $5,615
Adult Literacy: 99%
Life Expectancy (F): 79
Life Expectancy (M): 73

NORTHERN MARIANAS

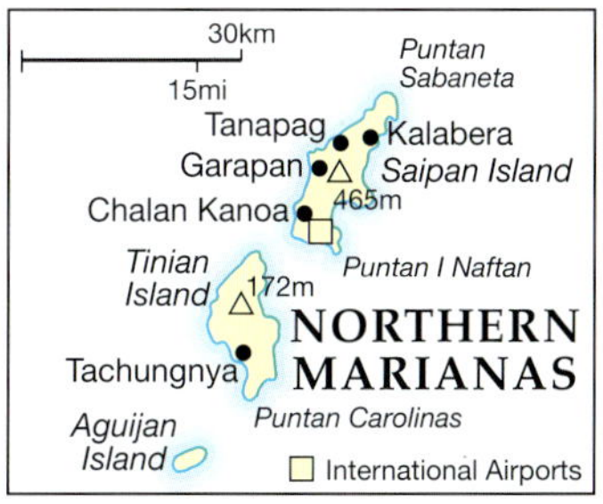

Facts and Figures

Capital: Saipan 38,900 (1990)
Area (sq km): 477
Population: 45.200 (1991)
Language: English, Chamorro
Religion: Roman Catholic
Currency: US Dollar
Annual Income per person: $3,500
Annual Trade per person: $10,000
Adult Literacy: 96%
Life Expectancy (F): 70
Life Expectancy (M): 65

89

PALAU

Facts and Figures

Capital: Koror 10,500 (1990)
Area (sq km): 488
Population: 15,200 (1990)
Language: Palaun, English
Religion: Roman Catholic
Currency: US Dollar
Annual Income per person: $2,550
Annual Trade per person: $1,922
Adult Literacy: Data not available
Life Expectancy (F): 74
Life Expectancy (M): 68

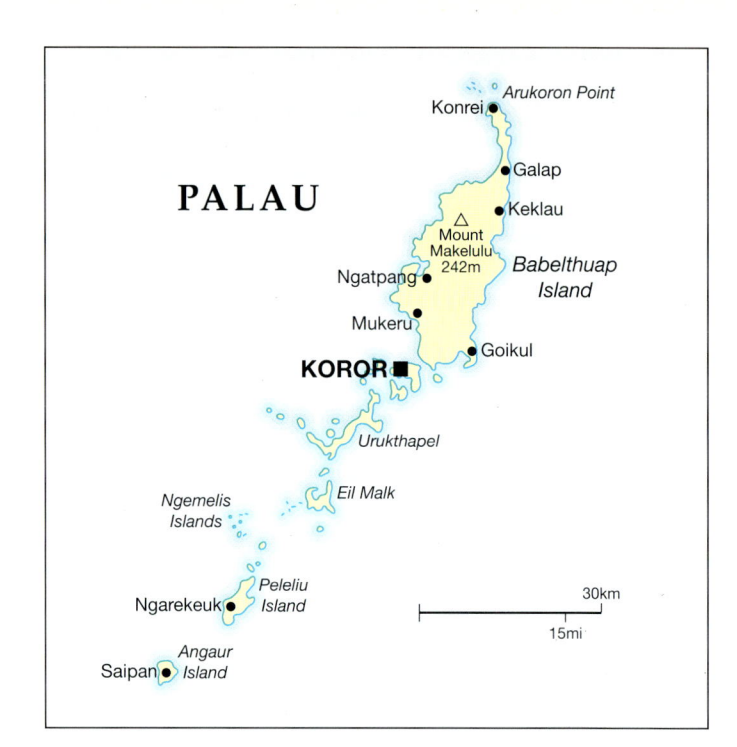

PALAU

- Arukoron Point
- Konrei
- Galap
- Keklau
- Mount Makelulu 242m
- Ngatpang
- Babelthuap Island
- Mukeru
- Goikul
- **KOROR**
- Urukthapel
- Eil Malk
- Ngemelis Islands
- Ngarekeuk
- Peleliu Island
- Saipan
- Angaur Island

PAPUA NEW GUINEA

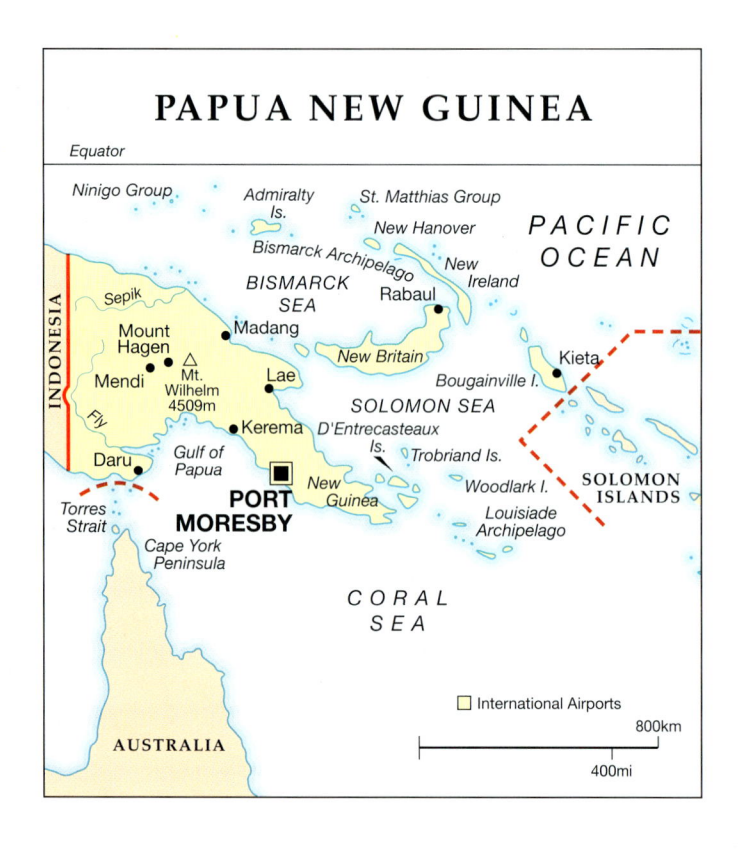

PAPUA NEW GUINEA

Equator

- Ninigo Group
- Admiralty Is.
- St. Matthias Group
- New Hanover
- Bismarck Archipelago
- New Ireland
- PACIFIC OCEAN
- Sepik
- BISMARCK SEA
- Rabaul
- INDONESIA
- Mount Hagen
- Madang
- New Britain
- Mendi
- Mt. Wilhelm 4509m
- Lae
- Kieta
- Kerema
- SOLOMON SEA
- Bougainville I.
- Fly
- D'Entrecasteaux Is.
- Trobriand Is.
- Daru
- Gulf of Papua
- New Guinea
- Woodlark I.
- SOLOMON ISLANDS
- **PORT MORESBY**
- Louisiade Archipelago
- Torres Strait
- Cape York Peninsula
- CORAL SEA
- AUSTRALIA

☐ International Airports

800km / 400mi

Facts and Figures

Capital: Port Moresby 193,300 (1990)
Area (sq km): 462,840
Population: 3,850,000 (1992)
Language: English, Aira Motu, Pidgin
Religion: Protestant 56% Roman Catholic 31% Traditional
Currency: Kina = 100 toea
Annual Income per person: $820
Annual Trade per person: $712
Adult Literacy: 52%
Life Expectancy (F): 57
Life Expectancy (M): 55

SOLOMON ISLANDS

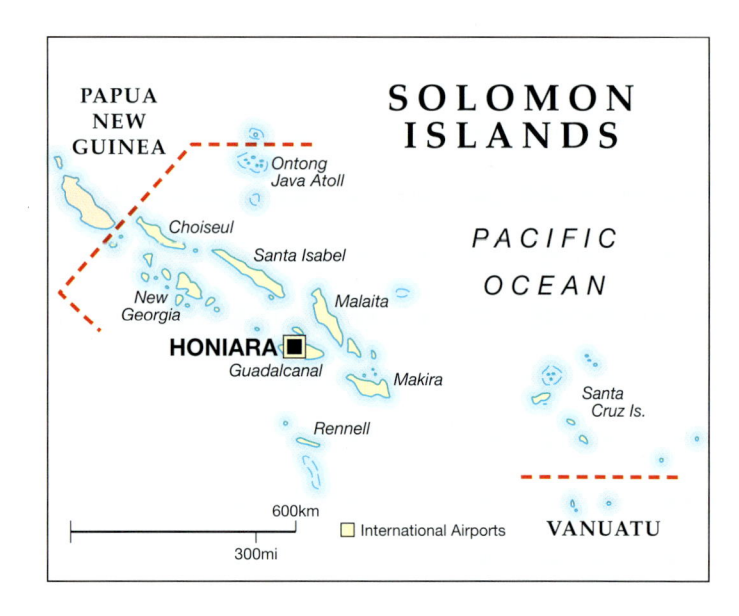

SOLOMON ISLANDS

- PAPUA NEW GUINEA
- Ontong Java Atoll
- Choiseul
- Santa Isabel
- PACIFIC OCEAN
- New Georgia
- Malaita
- **HONIARA**
- Guadalcanal
- Makira
- Santa Cruz Is.
- Rennell
- VANUATU

☐ International Airports

600km / 300mi

Facts and Figures

Capital: Honiara 33,800 (1989)
Area (sq km): 28,400
Population: 349,500 (1993)
Language: English, various Melanesian, Papuan and Polynesian languages
Religion: Protestant 75% Roman Catholic 19%
Currency: Solomon Is. Dollar = 100 cents
Annual Income per person: $560
Annual Trade per person: $506
Adult Literacy: 24%
Life Expectancy (F): 72
Life Expectancy (M): 67

TONGA

Facts and Figures

Capital: Nuku'alofa 29,000 (1986)
Area (sq km): 748
Population: 103,000 (1991)
Language: Tongan, English
Religion: Protestant 39%
Currency: Pa'anga = 100 seniti
Annual Income per person: $1,100
Annual Trade per person: $811
Adult Literacy: 99%
Life Expectancy (F): 70
Life Expectancy (M): 65

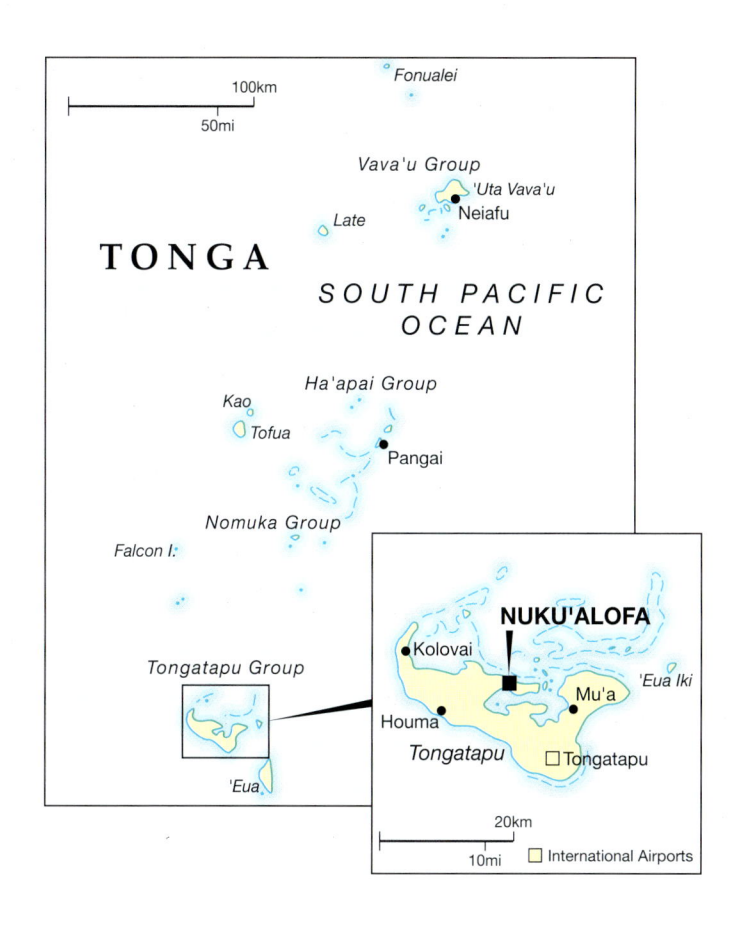

VANUATU

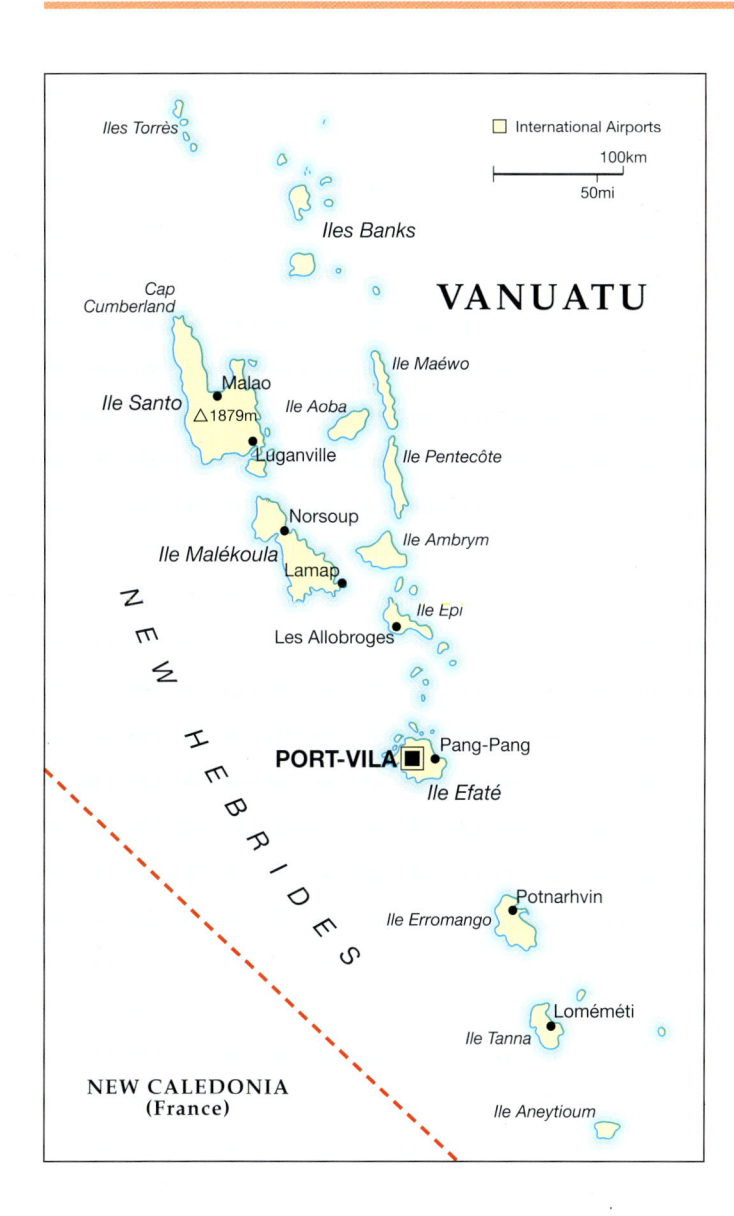

Facts and Figures

Capital: Port-Vila 19,400 (1989)
Area (sq km): 12,190
Population: 154,000 (1992)
Language: Bislama, English, French
Religion: Christian
Currency: Vatu = 100 centimes
Annual Income per person: $1,120
Annual Trade per person: $644
Adult Literacy: 67%
Life Expectancy (F): 72
Life Expectancy (M): 67

WESTERN SAMOA

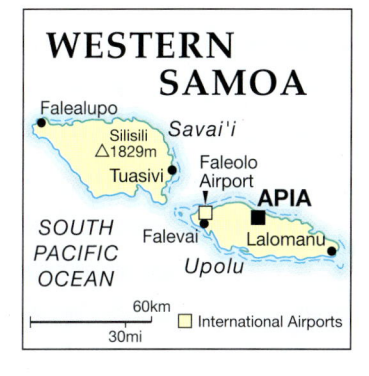

Facts and Figures

Capital: Apia 32,200 (1986)
Area (sq km): 2,830
Population: 168,000 (1990)
Language: Samoan, English
Religion: Protestant 62%
Roman Catholic 22%
Currency: Tala = 100 sene
Annual Income per person: $930
Annual Trade per person: $629
Adult Literacy: 92%
Life Expectancy (F): 69
Life Expectancy (M): 64

ARCTIC REGION

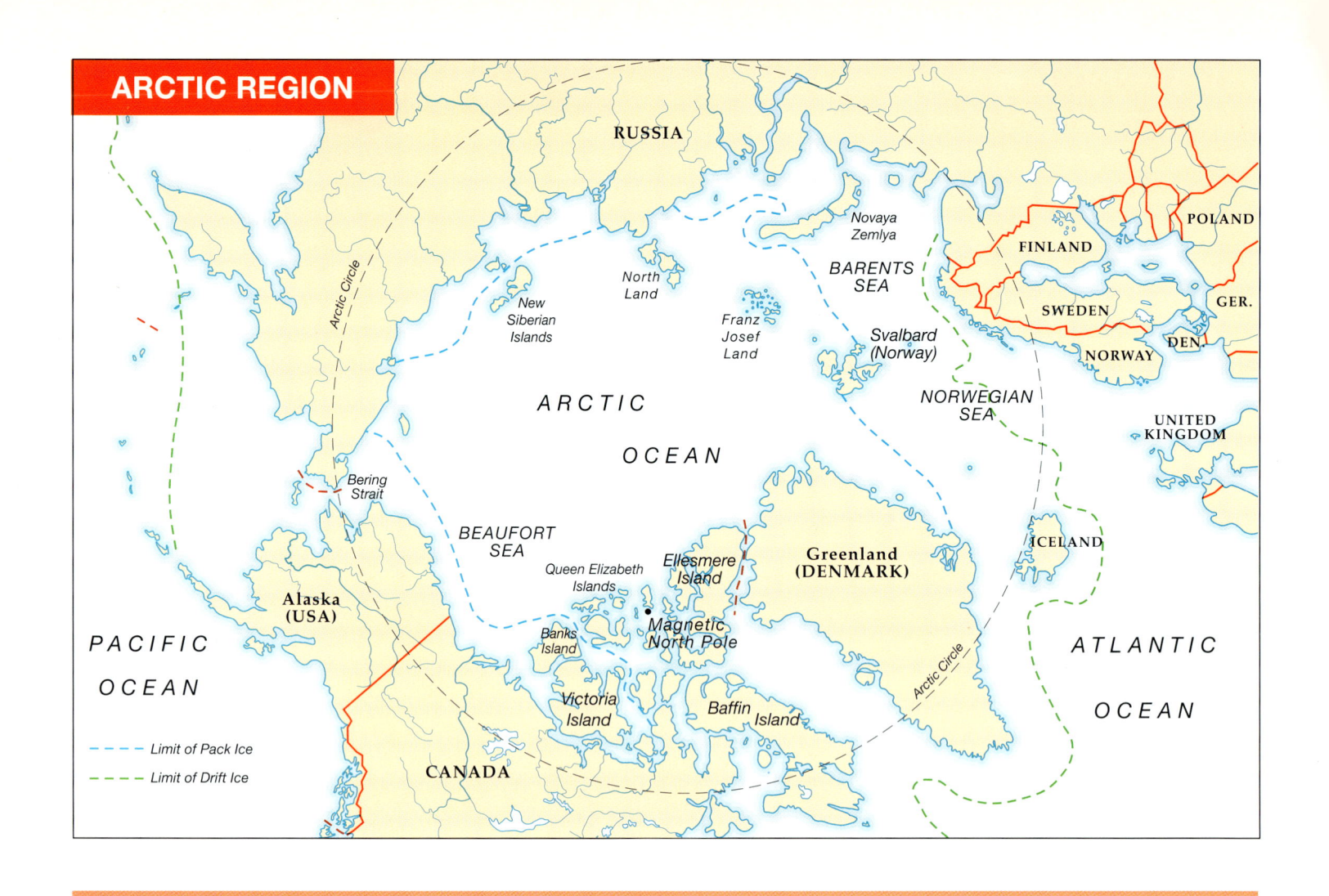

- - - Limit of Pack Ice
- - - Limit of Drift Ice

RUSSIA, Novaya Zemlya, North Land, New Siberian Islands, Franz Josef Land, BARENTS SEA, Svalbard (Norway), FINLAND, POLAND, SWEDEN, GER., DEN., NORWAY, NORWEGIAN SEA, UNITED KINGDOM, ARCTIC OCEAN, Arctic Circle, Bering Strait, BEAUFORT SEA, Queen Elizabeth Islands, Ellesmere Island, Greenland (DENMARK), ICELAND, ATLANTIC OCEAN, Alaska (USA), PACIFIC OCEAN, Banks Island, Magnetic North Pole, Victoria Island, Baffin Island, CANADA

ANTARCTICA

- - - Limit of Pack Ice
- - - Limit of Drift Ice

ATLANTIC OCEAN, Falkland Islands, ARGENTINA, CHILE, Antarctic Circle, BRITISH ANTARCTIC TERRITORY, Larsen Ice Shelf, Antarctic Peninsular, Ronne Ice Shelf, Queen Maud Land, NORWEGIAN DEPENDENCY, Amery Ice Shelf, AUSTRALIAN ANTARCTIC TERRITORY, Shackleton Ice Shelf, South Pole, Marie Byrd Land, Ross Ice Shelf, Wilkes Land, TERRE ADÉLIE (FRANCE), ROSS DEPENDENCY (NEW ZEALAND), Magnetic South Pole, PACIFIC OCEAN, INDIAN OCEAN

92

INDEX

A

Aachen Germany 21
Abadan Iran 74
Abéché Chad 53
Abeokuta Nigeria 62
Aberdeen United Kingdom 31
Aberystwyth United Kingdom 31
Abidjan Côte D'Ivoire 54
Abomey Benin 51
Abu Dhabi United Arab Emirates 85
Abu Kamal Syria 83
Abuja Nigeria 62
Acapulco Mexico 39
Accra Ghana 56
Acre Israel 75
Ada Ghana 56
Adana Turkey 29
Addis Ababa Ethiopia 55
Adelaide Australia 88
Aden Yemen 85
Adrar Algeria 50
Agadez Niger 62
Agadir Morocco 61
Agdam Azerbaijan 70
Agra India 74
Ahmadabad India 74
Ahvaz Iran 74
Ajman United Arab Emirates 85
Akmola Kazakhstan 77
Akranes Iceland 22
Akrotiri Cyprus 19
Aksum Ethiopia 55
Aktau Kazakhstan 77
Aktogay Kazakhstan 77
Aktyubinsk Kazakhstan 77
Akureyri Iceland 22
Al Ahmadi Kuwait 77
Al Ain United Arab Emirates 85
Al Basrah Iraq 75
Al Bayda Libya 58
Al Hasakah Syria 83
Al Jafr Jordan 76
Al Jahrah Kuwait 77
Al Khawr Qatar 81
Al Kufrah Libya 58
Al Kut Iraq 75
Al Wakrah Qatar 81
Alajuela Costa Rica 35
Alanya Turkey 29
Alaverdi Armenia 70
Ålborg Denmark 19
Albreda Gambia 56
Albuquerque United States 41
Ålesund Norway 26
Alexander Bay South Africa 64
Alexandria Egypt 55
Algiers Algeria 50
Ali-Sabieh Djibouti 54
Alicante Spain 28
Alice Springs Australia 88
All Saints Antigua & Barbuda 34
Alma-Ata Kazakhstan 77
Almería Spain 28
Alta Norway 26
Altyus Lithuania 24
Am Timan Chad 53
Ambohimanga Madagascar 59
Amiens France 20
Amman Jordan 76
Amritsar India 74
Amsterdam Netherlands 26
An Han Uzbekistan 85
An Najaf Iraq 75
Anabar Nauru 89
Anadyr Russia 82
Anchorage United States 41
Andermatt Switzerland 29
Andorra-la-Vella Andorra 16
Andros Town Bahamas 34
Aného Togo 65
Angekhakot Armenia 70
Angmagssalik Greenland 37
Angoche Mozambique 61
Angra do Heroismo Azores 50
Anibare Nauru 89
Ankara Turkey 29
Anna Nauru 89
Annaba Algeria 50
Antakya Turkey 29
Antalya Turkey 29
Antananarivo Madagascar 59
Antigua Guatemala 38
Antofagasta Chile 45
Antseranana Madagascar 59
Antwerp Belgium 17
Anuradhapura Sri Lanka 83
Aomori Japan 75
Apia Western Samoa 91
Apoteri Guyana 46
Aqaba Jordan 76
Arad Romania 27
Aralsk Kazakhstan 77
Ararat Armenia 70
Arbil Iraq 75
Arcalis Andorra 16
Arecibo Puerto Rico 40
Arequipa Peru 46
Argyle St Vincent 40
Århus Denmark 19
Arica Chile 45
Arima Trinidad & Tobago 41
Arkhangelsk Russia 82
Arlon Belgium 17
Armagh United Kingdom 31
Arnhem Netherlands 26
Arrecife Canary Islands 52
Arua Uganda 66
Arusha Tanzania 65
Aseb Eritrea 55
Ashkhabad Turkmenistan 84
Asmara Eritrea 55
Asunción Paraguay 46
Aswan Egypt 55
Atakpamé Togo 65
Atar Mauritania 60
Atbara Sudan 64
Atbasar Kazakhstan 77
Athens Greece 22
Athimatha Maldives 79
Atlanta United States 41
Atyrau Kazakhstan 77
Auckland New Zealand 89
Aveiro Portugal 27
Awali Bahrain 71
Awash Ethiopia 55
Ayorou Niger 62
Ayr United Kingdom 31
Azraq Jordan 76

B

Ba Fiji 88
Baalbek Lebanon 78
Bacolod Philippines 81
Badulla Sri Lanka 83
Bafatá Guinea Bissau 57
Baghdad Iraq 75
Baguio Philippines 81
Bahía Blanca Argentina 44
Bahlah Oman 80
Baikonur Kazakhstan 77
Bairiki Kiribati 88
Bakau Gambia 56
Bakel Senegal 63
Bakhtaran Iran 74
Baku Azerbaijan 70
Balikpapan Indonesia 74
Balkh Afghanistan 70
Balkhash Kazakhstan 77
Ballymena United Kingdom 31
Baltimore United States 41
Balzers Liechtenstein 24
Bamako Mali 60
Bambari Central African Republic 53
Bamiyan Afghanistan 70
Ban Hat Yai Thailand 84
Ban Houei Sai Laos 78
Ban Kantang Thailand 84
Ban Me Thuot Vietnam 85
Bandar Abbas Iran 74
Bandar Seri Begawan Brunei 72
Bandiagara Mali 60
Bangalore India 74
Bangar Brunei 72
Bangassou Central African Republic 53
Bangkok Thailand 84
Bangor United Kingdom 31
Bangui Central African Republic 53
Banja Luka Bosnia-Herzegovina 18
Banjul Gambia 56
Banská Bystrica Slovak Republic 27
Barahona Dominican Republic 37
Baranovichi Belarus 17
Barcelona Spain 28
Barcelona Venezuela 47
Bari Italy 23
Barmouth United Kingdom 31
Barquisimeto Venezuela 47
Barranquilla Colombia 45
Barrouallie St Vincent 40
Bartica Guyana 46
Basel Switzerland 29
Bassar Togo 65
Basse Santa Su Gambia 56
Basseterre St Christopher/Nevis 40
Bata Equatorial Guinea 55
Batavia Surinam 47
Bath United Kingdom 30
Bath St Christopher/Nevis 40
Batouri Cameroon 52
Battambang Cambodia 72
Batticaloa Sri Lanka 83
Batumi Georgia 72
Bauchi Nigeria 62
Bayamón Puerto Rico 40
Bayir Jordan 76
Bayonne France 20
Béchar Algeria 50
Beersheba Israel 75
Beijing China 73
Beira Mozambique 61
Beirut Lebanon 78
Beitbridge Zimbabwe 67
Beja Portugal 27
Bel'tsy Moldova 25
Beledweyne Somalia 64
Belém Brazil 44
Belfast United Kingdom 31
Belgrade Yugoslavia 29
Belize City Belize 35
Belleplaine Barbados 34
Belmopan Belize 35
Belo Horizonte Brazil 44
Benghazi Libya 58
Benguela Angola 50
Benin City Nigeria 62
Berat Albania 16
Berbera Somalia 64
Berbérati Central African Republic 53
Berekua Dominica 36
Bergen Norway 26
Bergen op Zoom Netherlands 26
Berlin Germany 21
Bern Switzerland 29
Bétaré Oya Cameroon 52
Beynau Kazakhstan 77
Bhadgaon Nepal 80
Biabou St Vincent 40
Bialystók Poland 26
Bihac Bosnia-Herzegovina 18
Bijeljina Bosnia-Herzegovina 18
Bilbao Spain 28
Bintulu Malaysia 78
Bir Moghrein Mauritania 60
Birao Central African Republic 53
Birjand Iran 74
Birkirkara Malta 25
Birmingham United Kingdom 30
Bishkek Kyrgyzstan 77
Bissau Guinea Bissau 57
Bitola Macedonia 25
Biumba Rwanda 62
Bizerta Tunisia 66
Blackmans Barbados 34
Blantyre Malawi 59
Bled Slovenia 28
Blida Algeria 50
Bloemfontein South Africa 64
Bluefields Nicaragua 39
Bo Sierra Leone 63
Boali Central African Republic 53
Bobo Dioulasso Burkina Faso 51
Bocaranga Central African Republic 53
Bodø Norway 26
Bogotá Colombia 45
Bogra Bangladesh 71
Boké Guinea 57
Bolama Guinea Bissau 57
Bolgatanga Ghana 56
Bologna Italy 23
Bombay India 74
Bondo Zaïre 66
Bongor Chad 53
Bonn Germany 21
Bonriki Kiribati 88
Bonthe Sierra Leone 63
Bordeaux France 20
Borzhomi Georgia 72
Bossango Central African Republic 53
Boston United States 41
Bouaké Côte D'Ivoire 54
Bouar Central African Republic 53
Boulogne France 20
Bourke Australia 88
Boutilimit Mauritania 60
Braga Portugal 27
Bragança Portugal 27
Brasilia Brazil 44
Brasov Romania 27
Bratislava Slovak Republic 27
Brazzaville Congo 54
Brecon United Kingdom 31
Bregenz Austria 16
Bremen Germany 21
Brest Belarus 17
Brezice Slovenia 28
Bridgetown Barbados 34
Brikama Gambia 56
Brindisi Italy 23
Brisbane Australia 88
Bristol United Kingdom 30
Brno Czech Republic 19
Broken Hill Australia 88
Broome Australia 88
Bruges Belgium 17
Brussels Belgium 17
Bubanza Burundi 52
Bucaramanga Colombia 45
Buchanan Liberia 58
Bucharest Romania 27
Budapest Hungary 22
Buenaventura Colombia 45
Buenos Aires Argentina 44
Builth Wells United Kingdom 31
Bujumbura Burundi 52
Bukavu Zaïre 66
Bukhara Uzbekistan 85
Bukit Panjang Singapore 83
Bulawayo Zimbabwe 67
Bura Kenya 57
Buraimi Oman 80
Burao Somalia 64
Burgas Bulgaria 18
Burgos Spain 28
Bursa Turkey 29
Bururi Burundi 52
Bushehr Iran 74
Butare Rwanda 62
Byblos Lebanon 78
Bydgoszcz Poland 26

C

Cabinda Angola 50
Cádiz Spain 28
Caernarfon United Kingdom 31
Cagayan de Oro Philippines 81
Cagliari Italy 23
Caguas Puerto Rico 40
Cairns Australia 88
Cairo Egypt 55
Cajamarca Peru 46
Calais France 20
Calcutta India 74
Calgary Canada 36
Cali Colombia 45
Callao Peru 46
Calliaqua St Vincent 40
Caluula Somalia 64
Cam Ranh Vietnam 85
Camagüey Cuba 36
Cambridge United Kingdom 30
Campo Grande Brazil 44
Can Tho Vietnam 85
Canaries St Lucia 40
Canberra Australia 88
Canchungo Guinea Bissau 57
Canillo Andorra 16
Cap Haïtien Haiti 38
Cape Coast Ghana 56
Cape Town South Africa 64
Caracas Venezuela 47
Cardiff United Kingdom 31
Cardigan United Kingdom 31
Cartagena Spain 28
Cartagena Colombia 45
Cartago Costa Rica 35
Casablanca Morocco 61
Castellón de la Plana Spain 28
Castelo Branco Portugal 27
Castle Bruce Dominica 36
Castries St Lucia 40
Catania Italy 23
Catio Guinea Bissau 57
Cayon St Christopher/Nevis 40
Cebu Philippines 81
Celje Slovenia 28
Ceské Budejovice Czech Republic 19
Ceuta Spain 28
Chalan Kanoa Northern Marianas 89
Chanea Greece 22
Changhua Taiwan 84
Changsha China 73
Chardzhou Turkmenistan 84
Charleroi Belgium 17
Charleston United States 41
Charlestown St Christopher/Nevis 40
Charleville Australia 88
Charlotte United States 41
Charlottetown Canada 36
Charlotteville Trinidad & Tobago 41
Chartres France 20
Chateaubelair St Vincent 40
Cheb Czech Republic 19
Cheju South Korea 76
Chelkar Kazakhstan 77
Chemnitz Germany 21
Chengde China 73
Chengdu China 73
Cherbourg France 20
Chernobyl Ukraine 29
Chiang Mai Thailand 84
Chiang Rai Thailand 84
Chibuto Mozambique 61
Chicago United States 41
Chiclayo Peru 46
Chihuahua Mexico 39
Chilumba Malawi 59
Chilung Taiwan 84
Chimkent Kazakhstan 77
Chimoio Mozambique 61
Chinandega Nicaragua 39
Chinde Mozambique 61
Chinguetti Mauritania 60
Chinhoyi Zimbabwe 67
Chipata Zambia 67
Chisinau Moldova 25
Chita Russia 82
Chittagong Bangladesh 71
Choiseul St Lucia 40
Choluteca Honduras 38
Chongjin North Korea 76
Chongqing China 73
Chonju South Korea 76
Choybalsan Mongolia 79
Christchurch New Zealand 89
Chu Kazakhstan 77
Chungju South Korea 76
Cienfuegos Cuba 36
Cincinnati United States 41
Ciudad Bolívar Venezuela 47
Ciudad Guayana Venezuela 47
Ciudad Real Spain 28
Clervaux Luxembourg 24
Clifton St Vincent 40
Cluj-Napoca Romania 27
Cobija Bolivia 44
Coca Ecuador 45
Cochabamba Bolivia 44
Cocoa Point Antigua & Barbuda 34
Codrington Antigua & Barbuda 34
Coimbra Portugal 27
Coleraine United Kingdom (N. Ireland) 31
Colombo Sri Lanka 83
Colón Panama 39
Colonarie St Vincent 40
Colwyn Bay United Kingdom (Wales) 31
Comilla Bangladesh 71
Comodoro Rivadavia Argentina 44
Conakry Guinea 57
Concepción Chile 45
Concepción Paraguay 46
Constanta Romania 27
Constantine Algeria 50
Copenhagen Denmark 19
Córdoba Spain 28
Córdoba Argentina 44
Corfu Greece 22
Corinto Nicaragua 39
Cork Ireland 23
Coro Venezuela 47
Corozal Belize 35
Cotonou Benin 51
Coulihaut Dominica 36
Coventry United Kingdom (England) 30
Covilhã Portugal 27
Cox's Bazar Bangladesh 71
Craiova Romania 27
Cristóbal Panama 39
Cruzeiro do Sul Brazil 44
Cuenca Ecuador 45
Cujda Morocco 61
Curepipe Mauritius 60
Cuttack India 74
Cyangugu Rwanda 62

D

Da Nang Vietnam 85
Daddato Djibouti 54
Dakar Senegal 63
Dakhla Western Sahara 61
Dalaman Turkey 29
Dalap-Uliga-Darrit Marshall Islands 89
Dalian China 73
Dallas United States 41
Daloa Côte D'Ivoire 54
Damman Saudi Arabia 82
Dangriga Belize 35
Dar es Salaam Tanzania 65
Dara Syria 83
Darhan Mongolia 79
Daru Papua New Guinea 90
Darwin Australia 88
Daugavpils Latvia 24
Davao Philippines 81
David Panama 39
Davos Switzerland 29
De Aar South Africa 64
Debar Macedonia 25
Debrecen Hungary 22
Delcovo Macedonia 25
Delgado El Salvador 37
Den Helder Netherlands 26
Dennery St Lucia 40
Denver United States 41
Derry United Kingdom 31
Detroit United States 41
Dhahran Saudi Arabia 82
Dhaka Bangladesh 71
Dhankuta Nepal 80
Dhekelia Cyprus 19
Dhiggiri Maldives 79
Dibrugarh India 74
Diekirch Luxembourg 24
Dieppe France 20
Dieppe Bay St Christopher/Nevis 40
Diffa Niger 62
Differdange Luxembourg 24
Dijon France 20
Dikhil Djibouti 54
Dilizhan Armenia 70
Dinajpur Bangladesh 71
Dinant Belgium 17
Diourbel Senegal 63
Dire Dawa Ethiopia 55
Djambala Congo 54
Djanet Algeria 50
Djenne Mali 60
Djibouti Djibouti 54
Djougou Benin 51
Dnepropetrovsk Ukraine 29
Dodoma Tanzania 65
Doha Qatar 81
Donegal Ireland 23
Donetsk Ukraine 29
Dongola Sudan 64
Dordrecht Netherlands 26
Dortmund Germany 21
Dosso Niger 62
Douala Cameroon 52
Dover United Kingdom 30
Dresden Germany 21
Drogheda Ireland 23
Druzhba Kazakhstan 77
Dubai United Arab Emirates 85
Dublin Ireland 23
Dubossary Moldova 25
Dubrovnik Croatia 18
Dudelange Luxembourg 24
Duisburg Germany 21
Dukhan Qatar 81
Dulcina Antigua & Barbuda 34
Dumfries United Kingdom 31
Dun Laoghaire Ireland 23
Dundalk Ireland 23
Dundas Greenland 37
Dundee United Kingdom 31
Dunedin New Zealand 89
Dunkwa Ghana 56
Durazno Uruguay 47
Durban South Africa 64
Durham United Kingdom 30
Durrës Albania 16
Dushanbe Tajikistan 84
Düsseldorf Germany 21
Dzhalal-Abad Kyrgyzstan 77
Dzhambul Kazakhstan 77
Dzhezkazgan Kazakhstan 77
Dzhusaly Kazakhstan 77

E

East London South Africa 64
Ebebiyin Equatorial Guinea 55
Echternach Luxembourg 24
Ed Eritrea 55
Edinburgh United Kingdom 31
Edirne Turkey 29
Edmonton Canada 36
Eilat Israel 75
Eindhoven Netherlands 26
Eita Kiribati 88
El Alamein Egypt 55
El Fasher Sudan 64
El Kharga Egypt 55
El Minya Egypt 55
El Obeid Sudan 64
El Paso United States 41
El Progreso Honduras 38
El Serrat Andorra 16
Elbasan Albania 16
Elblag Poland 26
Eldoret Kenya 57
Elmina Ghana 56
Emmen Netherlands 26
Encamp Andorra 16
Encarnación Paraguay 46
English Harbour Antigua & Barbuda 34
Enniskillen United Kingdom 31
Enschede Netherlands 26
Entebbe Uganda 66
Enugu Nigeria 62
Erdenet Mongolia 79
Erfurt Germany 21
Erzurum Turkey 29
Esbjerg Denmark 19
Esch-sur-Alzette Luxembourg 24
Eschen Liechtenstein 24
Escuintla Guatemala 38
Esfahan Iran 74
Esmeraldas Ecuador 45
Espoo Finland 21
Essen Germany 21
Ettelbrück Luxembourg 24
Évora Portugal 27
Exeter United Kingdom 30
Ezulwini Swaziland 65

F

Fada N'Gourma Burkina Faso 51
Fairbanks United States 41
Falealupo Western Samoa 91
Falevai Western Samoa 91
Falmouth Jamaica 39
Famagusta Cyprus 19

Fancy	St Vincent	40
Farah	Afghanistan	70
Faridpur	Bangladesh	71
Farim	Guinea Bissau	57
Faro	Portugal	27
Faya-Largeau	Chad	53
Fdérik	Mauritania	60
Felixstowe	United Kingdom	30
Fergana	Uzbekistan	85
Ferkessédougou	Côte D'Ivoire	54
Fez	Morocco	61
Fianarantsoa	Madagascar	59
Fier	Albania	16
Fiorentino	San Marino	23
Flatts Village	Bermuda	35
Florence	Italy	23
Flores	Guatemala	38
Folkestone	United Kingdom	30
Fontainebleau	France	20
Fontvieille	Monaco	20
Fort Shevchenko	Kazakhstan	77
Fort Worth	United States	41
Fortaleza	Brazil	44
Foumban	Cameroon	52
Francistown	Botswana	51
Frankfurt-am-Main	Germany	21
Fray Bentos	Uruguay	47
Fredericton	Canada	36
Frederikshåb	Greenland	37
Frederikshavn	Denmark	19
Freeport	Bahamas	34
Freetown	Sierra Leone	63
Fremantle	Australia	88
Fria	Guinea	57
Fuerte Olimpo	Paraguay	46
Fuerteventura	Canary Islands	52
Fujairah	United Arab Emirates	85
Fukuoka	Japan	75
Funafuti	Tuvalu	88
Funchal	Madeira	59
Fuzhou	China	73

G

Gaalkacyo	Somalia	64
Gabès	Tunisia	66
Gaborone	Botswana	51
Gabu	Guinea Bissau	57
Gafsa	Tunisia	66
Gagnoa	Côte D'Ivoire	54
Gagra	Georgia	72
Galap	Palau	90
Galati	Romania	27
Galle	Sri Lanka	83
Galway	Ireland	23
Gamboma	Congo	54
Gander	Canada	36
Ganta	Liberia	58
Gao	Mali	60
Garapan	Northern Marianas	89
Garoua	Cameroon	52
Gävle	Sweden	28
Gaza	Israel	75
Gaziantep	Turkey	29
Gbadolite	Zaïre	66
Gbarnga	Liberia	58
Gdansk	Poland	26
Gdynia	Poland	26
Geelong	Australia	88
Geneva	Switzerland	29
Genoa	Italy	23
George Town	Malaysia	78
Georgetown	St Vincent	40
Georgetown	Guyana	46
Georgetown	Gambia	56
Geraldton	Australia	88
Germiston	South Africa	64
Gevgelija	Macedonia	25
Ghadamis	Libya	58
Ghanzi	Botswana	51
Ghat	Libya	58
Ghazni	Afghanistan	70
Ghent	Belgium	17
Gibraltar	Spain	28
Gijón	Spain	28
Gisenye	Rwanda	62
Gitega	Burundi	52
Giurgiu	Romania	27
Giza	Egypt	55
Gjirokastër	Albania	16
Glasgow	United Kingdom	31
Goa	India	74
Gobabis	Namibia	61
Godhavn	Greenland	37
Godthåb	Greenland	37
Goiás	Brazil	44
Goikul	Palau	90
Gomel	Belarus	17
Gonaïves	Haiti	38
Gondar	Ethiopia	55
Gospic	Croatia	18
Göteborg	Sweden	28
Gouyave	Grenada	38
Governor's Harbour	Bahamas	34
Granada	Spain	28
Granada	Nicaragua	39
Grand Bassam	Côte D'Ivoire	54
Grand Roy	Grenada	38
Grande Anse	St Lucia	40
Grau-Roig	Andorra	16
Graz	Austria	16
Great Falls	United States	41
Greenville	Liberia	58
Greifswald	Germany	21
Grenoble	France	20
Grenville	Grenada	38
Grodno	Belarus	17
Groningen	Netherlands	26
Grootfontein	Namibia	61
Grøs Islets	St Lucia	40
Guadalajara	Mexico	39
Guanajuato	Mexico	39
Guangzhou	China	73
Guantanamo(US Base)	Cuba	36
Guatemala City	Guatemala	38
Guayaquil	Ecuador	45
Gullin	China	73
Gwadar	Pakistan	80
Gweru	Zimbabwe	67
Gyandzha	Azerbaijan	70
Györ	Hungary	22

H

Haapsalu	Estonia	20
Haarlem	Netherlands	26
Habban	Yemen	85
Hadiboh	Yemen	85
Haifa	Israel	75
Haiphong	Vietnam	85
Hajmah	Oman	80
Hakodate	Japan	75
Halab	Syria	83
Halba	Lebanon	78
Halifax	Canada	36
Halle	Germany	21
Hama	Syria	83
Hamadan	Iran	74
Hambantota	Sri Lanka	83
Hamburg	Germany	21
Hämeenlinna	Finland	21
Hamhung	North Korea	76
Hamilton	Bermuda	35
Hamilton	Canada	36
Hamilton	New Zealand	89
Hammamet	Tunisia	66
Hammerfest	Norway	26
Hangzhou	China	73
Hannover	Germany	21
Hanoi	Vietnam	85
Harar	Ethiopia	55
Harare	Zimbabwe	67
Harbin	China	73
Hargeysa	Somalia	64
Harper	Liberia	58
Harwich	United Kingdom	30
Hassi Messaoud	Algeria	50
Hastings	Barbados	34
Havana	Cuba	36
Hebron	Israel	75
Helsingborg	Sweden	28
Helsingør	Denmark	19
Helsinki	Finland	21
Henzada	Myanmar	79
Herakleion	Greece	22
Herat	Afghanistan	70
Heredia	Costa Rica	35
Hermel	Lebanon	78
Hillsborough	Grenada	38
Hiroshima	Japan	75
Hlatikulu	Swaziland	65
Ho	Ghana	56
Ho Chi Minh City	Vietnam	85
Hobart	Australia	88
Hobyo	Somalia	64
Hodeida	Yemen	85
Hoek van Holland	Netherlands	26
Höfn	Iceland	22
Hofuf	Saudi Arabia	82
Holetown	Barbados	34
Holguin	Cuba	36
Holon	Israel	75
Holyhead	United Kingdom	31
Homs	Syria	83
Hong Kong	Hong Kong	73
Honiara	Solomon Islands	90
Honolulu	United States	41
Horta	Azores	50
Houma	Tonga	91
Houston	United States	41
Hovd	Mongolia	79
Hsinchu	Taiwan	84
Hualien	Taiwan	84
Huambo	Angola	50
Hue	Vietnam	85
Hull	United Kingdom	30
Humacao	Puerto Rico	40
Hungnam	North Korea	76
Hurghada	Egypt	55
Hwange	Zimbabwe	67
Hyderabad	India	74
Hyderabad	Pakistan	80

I

Iasi	Romania	27
Ibadan	Nigeria	62
Ibiza	Balearic Is.	17
Ibri	Oman	80
Ica	Peru	46
Ifni	Morocco	61
Iguatu	Brazil	44
Iloilo	Philippines	81
Ilorin	Nigeria	62
Impfondo	Congo	54
In Salah	Algeria	50
Inchon	South Korea	76
Independence	Belize	35
Indore	India	74
Inhambane	Mozambique	61
Innsbruck	Austria	16
Interlaken	Switzerland	29
Invercargill	New Zealand	89
Inverness	United Kingdom	31
Iquitos	Peru	46
Iranshahr	Iran	74
Irbid	Jordan	76
Iringa	Tanzania	65
Irkutsk	Russia	82
Isafjördhur	Iceland	22
Iskenderun	Turkey	29
Islamabad	Pakistan	80
Istanbul	Turkey	29
Ita	Paraguay	46
Izmir	Turkey	29

J

Jackson	United States	41
Jacmel	Haiti	38
Jaffa	Israel	75
Jaffna	Sri Lanka	83
Jaipur	India	74
Jakarta	Indonesia	74
Jakobshavn	Greenland	37
Jalalabad	Afghanistan	70
Jarabulus	Syria	83
Jayapura	Indonesia	74
Jeddah	Saudi Arabia	82
Jelgava	Latvia	24
Jérémie	Haiti	38
Jericho	Israel	75
Jerusalem	Israel	75
Jimma	Ethiopia	55
Jinan	China	73
Jinja	Uganda	66
Joensuu	Finland	21
Johannesburg	South Africa	64
Johor Baharu	Malaysia	78
Jönköping	Sweden	28
Juba	Sudan	64
Jubayl	Saudi Arabia	82
Juneau	United States	41
Jurmala	Latvia	24
Jurong	Singapore	83
Juticalpa	Honduras	38
Jwaneng	Botswana	51
Jyväskylä	Finland	21

K

Kabala	Sierra Leone	63
Kabale	Uganda	66
Kabarole	Uganda	66
Kabul	Afghanistan	70
Kabwe	Zambia	67
Kadoma	Zimbabwe	67
Kaduna	Nigeria	62
Kaédi	Mauritania	60
Kaesong	North Korea	76
Kagul	Moldova	25
Kairouan	Tunisia	66
Kalabera	Northern Marianas	89
Kalai Mor	Turkmenistan	84
Kalgoorlie	Australia	88
Kalomo	Zambia	67
Kalutara	Sri Lanka	83
Kamo	Armenia	70
Kampala	Uganda	66
Kananga	Zaïre	66
Kandahar	Afghanistan	70
Kandy	Sri Lanka	83
Kangnung	South Korea	76
Kankan	Guinea	57
Kano	Nigeria	62
Kanpur	India	74
Kansas City	United States	41
Kanye	Botswana	51
Kaohsiung	Taiwan	84
Kaolack	Senegal	63
Karachi	Pakistan	80
Karaganda	Kazakhstan	77
Karak	Jordan	76
Karasburg	Namibia	61
Karaudanawa	Guyana	46
Karibib	Namibia	61
Karlovac	Croatia	18
Karlstad	Sweden	28
Karonga	Malawi	59
Kars	Turkey	29
Kasama	Zambia	67
Kasane	Botswana	51
Kashi	China	73
Kassala	Sudan	64
Kassel	Germany	21
Kasserine	Tunisia	66
Kasungu	Malawi	59
Kathmandu	Nepal	80
Katong	Singapore	83
Katowice	Poland	26
Kaunas	Lithuania	24
Kawasaki	Japan	75
Kayes	Mali	60
Kazanluk	Bulgaria	18
Kecskemét	Hungary	22
Kédougou	Senegal	63
Keetmanshoop	Namibia	61
Keflavik	Iceland	22
Keklau	Palau	90
Kenema	Sierra Leone	63
Kenitra	Morocco	61
Kenting	Taiwan	84
Kerema	Papua New Guinea	90
Kerewan	Gambia	56
Kerki	Turkmenistan	84
Kerman	Iran	74
Khabarovsk	Russia	82
Kharkov	Ukraine	29
Khartoum	Sudan	64
Khiva	Uzbekistan	85
Khodzheni	Tajikistan	84
Khon Kaen	Thailand	84
Khor Fakkan	United Arab Emirates	85
Khorog	Tajikistan	84
Khulna	Bangladesh	71
Khutse	Botswana	51
Kibungu	Rwanda	62
Kibuye	Rwanda	62
Kicevo	Macedonia	25
Kiel	Germany	21
Kieta	Papua New Guinea	90
Kiov	Ukraine	29
Kigali	Rwanda	62
Kigoma	Tanzania	65
Kikwit	Zaïre	66
Kilkenny	Ireland	23
Killarney	Ireland	23
Kilwe Kisiwani	Tanzania	65
Kimberley	South Africa	64
Kimchaek	North Korea	76
Kindia	Guinea	57
Kingston	Jamaica	39
Kingstown	St Vincent	40
Kinshasa	Zaïre	66
Kipili	Tanzania	65
Kirkuk	Iraq	75
Kirovakan	Armenia	70
Kiruna	Sweden	28
Kisangani	Zaïre	66
Kismaayo	Somalia	64
Kisumu	Kenya	57
Kitakyushu	Japan	75
Kitale	Kenya	57
Kitgum	Uganda	66
Kitwe	Zambia	67
Kizyl Arvat	Turkmenistan	84
Klagenfurt	Austria	16
Klaipeda	Lithuania	24
Knock	Ireland	23
Kobe	Japan	75
Kocani	Macedonia	25
Koforidua	Ghana	56
Kohtla-Järve	Estonia	20
Kokand	Uzbekistan	85
Kokchetav	Kazakhstan	77
Kolding	Denmark	19
Köln	Germany	21
Kolovai	Tonga	91
Kompong Cham	Cambodia	72
Kompong Chhnang	Cambodia	72
Kompong Som	Cambodia	72
Kompong Thom	Cambodia	72
Komsomolsk-na-Amure	Russia	82
Konrei	Palau	90
Konya	Turkey	29
Koper	Slovenia	28
Korçë	Albania	16
Korhogo	Côte D'Ivoire	54
Koror	Palau	90
Kos	Greece	22
Kosice	Slovak Republic	27
Kosti	Sudan	64
Koszalin	Poland	26
Kota Kinabalu	Malaysia	78
Koudougou	Burkina Faso	51
Kouroussa	Guinea	57
Kowloon	Hong Kong	73
Kozina	Slovenia	28
Kpalimé	Togo	65
Kraków	Poland	26
Kranj	Slovenia	28
Kranji	Singapore	83
Krasnovodsk	Turkmenistan	84
Krasnoyarsk	Russia	82
Kribi	Cameroon	52
Krishnanagar	Bangladesh	71
Kristiansand	Norway	26
Kristiansund	Norway	26
Krujë	Albania	16
Kuala Belait	Brunei	72
Kuala Lumpur	Malaysia	78
Kuala Terengganu	Malaysia	78
Kuba	Azerbaijan	70
Kuching	Malaysia	78
Kukës	Albania	16
Kulsary	Kazakhstan	77
Kulyab	Tajikistan	84
Kumanovo	Macedonia	25
Kumasi	Ghana	56
Kumayri	Armenia	70
Kunfunadhoo	Maldives	79
Kunming	China	73
Kunsan	South Korea	76
Kuopio	Finland	21
Kuredhdhu	Maldives	79
Kuressaare	Estonia	20
Kurgan-Tyube	Tajikistan	84
Kurunegala	Sri Lanka	83
Kustanay	Kazakhstan	77
Kutaisi	Georgia	72
Kuwait City	Kuwait	77
Kwangju	South Korea	76
Kwekwe	Zimbabwe	67
Kyongju	South Korea	76
Kyoto	Japan	75
Kyrenia	Cyprus	19
Kzyl-Orda	Kazakhstan	77

L

La Ceiba	Honduras	38
La Condamine	Monaco	20
La Paz	Mexico	39
La Paz	Bolivia	44
La Plaine	Dominica	36
La Plata	Argentina	44
La Romana	Dominican Republic	37
La Serena	Chile	45
La Union	El Salvador	37
La Vega	Dominican Republic	37
La'youne	Western Sahara	61
Labasa	Fiji	88
Labé	Guinea	57
Laborie	St Lucia	40
Lae	Papua New Guinea	90
Laghouat	Algeria	50
Lagos	Portugal	27
Lagos	Nigeria	62
Lahore	Pakistan	80
Lahti	Finland	21
Lalibela	Ethiopia	55
Lalomanu	Western Samoa	91
Lamap	Vanuatu	91
Lambaréné	Gabon	56
Lanzhou	China	73
Lao Cai	Vietnam	85
Laoag	Philippines	81
Larisa	Greece	22
Larnaca	Cyprus	19
Larne	United Kingdom	31
Las Palmas	Canary Islands	52
Las Vegas	United States	41
Lashio	Myanmar	79
Lastoursville	Gabon	56
Latakia	Syria	83
Lausanne	Switzerland	29
Lavumisa	Swaziland	65
Layou	St Vincent	40
Le Havre	France	20
Leeds	United Kingdom	30
Leeuwarden	Netherlands	26
Lefka	Cyprus	19
Legoland	Denmark	19
Leiden	Netherlands	26
Leipzig	Germany	21
Lenkoran	Azerbaijan	70
León	Nicaragua	39
Leribe	Lesotho	58
Les Allobroges	Vanuatu	91
Les Cayes	Haiti	38
Les Escaldes	Andorra	16
Lesbos	Greece	22
Leticia	Colombia	45
Levuka	Fiji	88
Lezhë	Albania	16
Lhasa	China	73
Libenge	Zaïre	66
Liberec	Czech Republic	19
Liberia	Costa Rica	35
Libreville	Gabon	56
Lichinga	Mozambique	61
Liège	Belgium	17
Liepaja	Latvia	24
Likasi	Zaïre	66
Lille	France	20
Lilongwe	Malawi	59
Lima	Peru	46
Limassol	Cyprus	19
Limbe	Cameroon	52
Limbe	Malawi	59
Limerick	Ireland	23
Limoges	France	20
Limón	Costa Rica	35
Linden	Guyana	46
Lindi	Tanzania	65
Linguère	Senegal	63
Linz	Austria	16
Lisbon	Portugal	27
Lisburn	United Kingdom	31
Liverpool	United Kingdom	30
Livno	Bosnia-Herzegovina	18
Ljubljana	Slovenia	28
Ljuw	Nauru	89
Lobamba	Swaziland	65
Lobatse	Botswana	51
Lobito	Angola	50
Lodwar	Kenya	57
Lodz	Poland	26
Loja	Ecuador	45
Lomé	Togo	65
Loméméti	Vanuatu	91
London	United Kingdom	30
London	Kiribati	88
Longreach	Australia	88
Los Angeles	United States	41
Loubomo	Congo	54
Luanda	Angola	50
Luang-Phrabang	Laos	78
Luba	Equatorial Guinea	55
Lubango	Angola	50
Lübeck	Germany	21
Lublin	Poland	26
Lubumbashi	Zaïre	66
Lucknow	India	74
Lüderitz	Namibia	61
Luena	Angola	50
Lugano	Switzerland	29
Luganville	Vanuatu	91
Lunsar	Sierra Leone	63
Lusaka	Zambia	67
Luuq	Somalia	64
Luxembourg	Luxembourg	24
Luxor	Egypt	55
Luzern	Switzerland	29
Lvov	Ukraine	29
Lyon	France	20

M

Ma'an	Jordan	76
Maastricht	Netherlands	26
Machakos	Kenya	57
Machala	Ecuador	45
Madang	Papua New Guinea	90
Madhah	Oman	80
Madras	India	74
Madrid	Spain	28
Mafeteng	Lesotho	58
Mafraq	Jordan	76
Magadan	Russia	82
Magdeburg	Germany	21
Mahajanga	Madagascar	59
Mahébourg	Mauritius	60
Mahón	Balearic Is.	17
Maiduguri	Nigeria	62
Makarska	Croatia	18
Makeni	Sierra Leone	63
Makokou	Gabon	56
Malabo	Equatorial Guinea	55
Málaga	Spain	28
Malakal	Sudan	64
Malanje	Angola	50
Malaren	Sweden	28
Malé	Maldives	79
Malindi	Kenya	57
Malmö	Sweden	28
Man	Côte D'Ivoire	54
Manacor	Balearic Is.	17
Manado	Indonesia	74
Managua	Nicaragua	39
Manama	Bahrain	71
Manaus	Brazil	44
Manchester	United Kingdom	30
Mandalay	Myanmar	79
Mandeville	Jamaica	39
Mango	Togo	65
Mangot	Dominica	36
Manila	Philippines	81
Mankayane	Swaziland	65
Manokwari	Indonesia	74
Mansa	Zambia	67
Mansoa	Guinea Bissau	57
Manta	Ecuador	45
Manzini	Swaziland	65
Maputo	Mozambique	61
Mar del Plata	Argentina	44
Maracaibo	Venezuela	47
Maradi	Niger	62
Marakabeis	Lesotho	58
Maramba	Zambia	67
Maribor	Slovenia	28
Mariental	Namibia	61
Marigot	St Lucia	40
Mariscal Estigarribia	Paraguay	46
Marka	Somalia	64
Maroua	Cameroon	52

Marquis	St Lucia	40
Marrakech	Morocco	61
Marsabit	Kenya	57
Marsaxlokk	Malta	25
Marseille	France	20
Mary	Turkmenistan	84
Masaka	Uganda	66
Masan	South Korea	76
Masaya	Nicaragua	39
Maseru	Lesotho	58
Mashhad	Iran	74
Masindi	Uganda	66
Massawa	Eritrea	55
Masuku	Gabon	56
Masvingo	Zimbabwe	67
Matadi	Zaïre	66
Matagalpa	Nicaragua	39
Matam	Senegal	63
Matara	Sri Lanka	83
Matrah	Oman	80
Matrûh	Egypt	55
Matthew Town	Bahamas	34
Maun	Botswana	51
Maura	Brunei	72
Mauren	Liechtenstein	24
Mavinga	Angola	50
Mayagüez	Puerto Rico	40
Mayumba	Gabon	56
Mazar-i-Sharif	Afghanistan	70
Mazatenango	Guatemala	38
Mazeikiai	Lithuania	24
Mbabane	Swaziland	65
Mbala	Zambia	67
Mbale	Uganda	66
Mbandaka	Zaïre	66
Mbé	Congo	54
Mbeya	Tanzania	65
Mbuji-Mayi	Zaïre	66
Mdina	Malta	25
Mecca	Saudi Arabia	82
Mechelen	Belgium	17
Medellín	Colombia	45
Medenine	Tunisia	66
Medina	Saudi Arabia	82
Megri	Armenia	70
Mejicanos	El Salvador	37
Meknès	Morocco	61
Melaka	Malaysia	78
Melbourne	Australia	88
Melilla	Spain	28
Melo	Uruguay	47
Memphis	United States	41
Mendi	Papua New Guinea	90
Mendoza	Argentina	44
Menongue	Angola	50
Mercedes	Uruguay	47
Mergui	Myanmar	79
Mérida	Mexico	39
Mérida	Venezuela	47
Mersin	Turkey	29
Merthyr Tydfil	United Kingdom	31
Mesters Vig	Greenland	37
Mexicali	Mexico	39
Mexico City	Mexico	39
Miami	United States	41
Micoud	St Lucia	40
Milan	Italy	23
Milford Haven	United Kingdom	31
Milwaukee	United States	41
Mina al Ahmadi	Kuwait	77
Mina Saud	Kuwait	77
Mina Sulman	Bahrain	71
Minas	Uruguay	47
Mindelo	Cape Verde	53
Mingyan	Myanmar	79
Minneapolis	United States	41
Minsk	Belarus	17
Miskolc	Hungary	22
Misratah	Libya	58
Mitu	Colombia	45
Mitzic	Gabon	56
Moçambique	Mozambique	61
Mochudi	Botswana	51
Moengo	Surinam	47
Mogadishu	Somalia	64
Mogilev	Belarus	17
Mohales Hoek	Lesotho	58
Mokha	Yemen	85
Mokhotlong	Lesotho	58
Mokolo	Cameroon	52
Mokpo	South Korea	76
Moldovita	Romania	27
Mollendo	Peru	46
Mombasa	Kenya	57
Monaco	Monaco	20
Monastir	Tunisia	66
Mongo	Chad	53
Monkey Bay	Malawi	59
Monrovia	Liberia	58
Mons	Belgium	17
Monte Carlo	Monaco	20
Montego Bay	Jamaica	39
Monterrey	Mexico	39
Montevideo	Uruguay	47
Montréal	Canada	36
Montreux	Switzerland	29
Mopti	Mali	60
Morogoro	Tanzania	65
Morondava	Madagascar	59
Moroni	Comoros	54
Moroto	Uganda	66
Moruga	Trinidad & Tobago	41
Moscow	Russia	82
Moshi	Tanzania	65
Mosta	Malta	25
Mostaganem	Algeria	50
Mostar	Bosnia-Herzegovina	18
Mosul	Iraq	75
Moulmein	Myanmar	79
Moundou	Chad	53
Mount Darwin	Zimbabwe	67
Mount Hagen	Papua New Guinea	90
Mount Isa	Australia	88
Moyale	Kenya	57
Mozyr	Belarus	17
Mtwara	Tanzania	65
Mu'a	Tonga	91
Mufulira	Zambia	67
Muharraq	Bahrain	71
Mukalla	Yemen	85
Mukeru	Palau	90
Mullaittivu	Sri Lanka	83
Multan	Pakistan	80
München	Germany	21
Münster	Germany	21
Muramvya	Burundi	52
Murcia	Spain	28
Murgab	Tajikistan	84
Murmansk	Russia	82
Muscat	Oman	80
Mutare	Zimbabwe	67
Muyinga	Burundi	52
Mwanza	Tanzania	65
Myitkyina	Myanmar	79
Mymensingh	Bangladesh	71
Mzuzu	Malawi	59

N

N'Djaména	Chad	53
N'kayi	Congo	54
Nablus	Israel	75
Nacala	Mozambique	61
Nadi	Fiji	88
Nagasaki	Japan	75
Nagoya	Japan	75
Nagpur	India	74
Nairobi	Kenya	57
Najran	Saudi Arabia	82
Nakhichevan	Azerbaijan	70
Nakhon Ratchasima	Thailand	84
Nakhon Sawan	Thailand	84
Nakhon Si Thammarat	Thailand	84
Nakuru	Kenya	57
Namangan	Uzbekistan	85
Namibe	Angola	50
Nampo	North Korea	76
Nampula	Mozambique	61
Namur	Belgium	17
Nanchang	China	73
Nancy	France	20
Nanjing	China	73
Nanning	China	73
Nantes	France	20
Napier	New Zealand	89
Naples	Italy	23
Narayanganj	Bangladesh	71
Narsarsuaq	Greenland	37
Narva	Estonia	20
Narvik	Norway	26
Naryn	Kyrgyzstan	77
Nashville	United States	41
Nassau	Bahamas	34
Natitingou	Benin	51
Nausori	Fiji	88
Nazareth	Israel	75
Nazca	Peru	46
Nazwa	Oman	80
Ndjole	Gabon	56
Ndola	Zambia	67
Nebit-Dag	Turkmenistan	84
Negombo	Sri Lanka	83
Negril	Jamaica	39
Neiafu	Tonga	91
Nelson	New Zealand	89
Néma	Mauritania	60
Nendeln	Liechtenstein	24
Neuchâtel	Switzerland	29
New Amsterdam	Guyana	46
New Delhi	India	74
New Orleans	United States	41
New Sandy Bay	St Vincent	40
New Tamale	Ghana	56
New York	United States	41
Newcastle	United Kingdom	30
Newcastle	St Christopher/Nevis	40
Newcastle	Australia	88
Newhaven	United Kingdom	30
Newport	United Kingdom	31
Newry	United Kingdom	31
Ngaoundéré	Cameroon	52
Ngarekeuk	Palau	90
Ngatpang	Palau	90
Ngozi	Burundi	52
Nha Trang	Vietnam	85
Nhlangano	Swaziland	65
Niamey	Niger	62
Nice	France	20
Nicosia	Cyprus	19
Nicoya	Costa Rica	35
Niefang	Equatorial Guinea	55
Nieuw Nickerie	Surinam	47
Nikolayev	Ukraine	29
Nis	Yugoslavia	29
Nisab	Yemen	85
Nitra	Slovak Republic	27
Nizhny Novgorod	Russia	82
Nkongsamba	Cameroon	52
Norrköping	Sweden	28
Norsoup	Vanuatu	91
Norwich	United Kingdom	30
Nouadhibou	Mauritania	60
Nouakchott	Mauritania	60
Novabad	Tajikistan	84
Novosibirsk	Russia	82
Nuku'alofa	Tonga	91
Nukus	Uzbekistan	85
Nürnberg	Germany	21
Nushki	Pakistan	80
Nuwara Eliya	Sri Lanka	83
Nzérékoré	Guinea	57

O

Oaxaca	Mexico	39
Oban	United Kingdom	31
Obock	Djibouti	54
Obuasi	Ghana	56
Ocho Rios	Jamaica	39
Odense	Denmark	19
Odessa	Ukraine	29
Odienné	Côte D'Ivoire	54
Ogbomosho	Nigeria	62
Ohrid	Macedonia	25
Okha	Russia	82
Okhotsk	Russia	82
Old Road	St Christopher/Nevis	40
Olinda	Brazil	44
Olomouc	Czech Republic	19
Omdurman	Sudan	64
Omsk	Russia	82
Oporto	Portugal	27
Oradea	Romania	27
Oran	Algeria	50
Orange Walk	Belize	35
Oranjemund	Namibia	61
Orapa	Botswana	51
Ordino	Andorra	16
Örebro	Sweden	28
Orgeyev	Moldova	25
Orlando	United States	41
Orsha	Belarus	17
Oruro	Bolivia	44
Osaka	Japan	75
Osh	Kyrgyzstan	77
Oshogbo	Nigeria	62
Osijek	Croatia	18
Oslo	Norway	26
Ostend	Belgium	17
Östersund	Sweden	28
Ostrava	Czech Republic	19
Oswiecim	Poland	26
Ottawa	Canada	36
Ouagadougou	Burkina Faso	51
Ouahigouya	Burkina Faso	51
Ouargla	Algeria	50
Ouesso	Congo	54
Ouidah	Benin	51
Oulu	Finland	21
Owando	Congo	54
Oxford	United Kingdom	30
Oyo	Nigeria	62

P

Padang	Indonesia	74
Pagan	Myanmar	79
Pakse	Laos	78
Pal	Andorra	16
Palapye	Botswana	51
Palembang	Indonesia	74
Palermo	Italy	23
Palma	Balearic Is.	17
Palmerston North	New Zealand	89
Panama City	Panama	39
Panevezys	Lithuania	24
Pang-Pang	Vanuatu	91
Pangai	Tonga	91
Paphos	Cyprus	19
Paraguari	Paraguay	46
Parakou	Benin	51
Paramaribo	Surinam	47
Pardubice	Czech Republic	19
Paris	France	20
Paris	Kiribati	88
Pärnu	Estonia	20
Paro	Bhutan	71
Pas de la Casa	Andorra	16
Pasto	Colombia	45
Patan	Nepal	80
Patras	Greece	22
Pattaya	Thailand	84
Paviodar	Kazakhstan	77
Paysandú	Uruguay	47
Pécs	Hungary	22
Pedra Lume	Cape Verde	53
Pegu	Myanmar	79
Pemba	Mozambique	61
Perth	United Kingdom	31
Perth	Australia	88
Pescara	Italy	23
Peshawar	Pakistan	80
Petaling Jaya	Malaysia	78
Petit Loango	Gabon	56
Petropavlovsk	Kazakhstan	77
Philadelphia	United States	41
Phitsanulok	Thailand	84
Phnom Penh	Cambodia	72
Phoenix	United States	41
Phuket	Thailand	84
Phuntsholing	Bhutan	71
Pietermaritzburg	South Africa	64
Pigg's Peak	Swaziland	65
Pilar	Paraguay	46
Pinsk	Belarus	17
Piraeus	Greece	22
Piran	Slovenia	28
Pisa	Italy	23
Piteå	Sweden	28
Pittsburgh	United States	41
Pleven	Bulgaria	18
Plitvice	Croatia	18
Ploiesti	Romania	27
Plovdiv	Bulgaria	18
Plymouth	United Kingdom	30
Plzen	Czech Republic	19
Podgorica	Yugoslavia	29
Point Fortin	Trinidad & Tobago	41
Pointe-Noire	Congo	54
Pokhara	Nepal	80
Polonnaruwa	Sri Lanka	83
Polotsk	Belarus	17
Poltava	Ukraine	29
Ponce	Puerto Rico	40
Ponta Delgada	Azores	50
Pontianak	Indonesia	74
Pontoetoe	Surinam	47
Pori	Finland	21
Port Antonio	Jamaica	39
Port Augusta	Australia	88
Port Elizabeth	St Vincent	40
Port Elizabeth	South Africa	64
Port Gentil	Gabon	56
Port Harcourt	Nigeria	62
Port Kaituma	Guyana	46
Port Louis	Mauritius	60
Port Moresby	Papua New Guinea	90
Port of Spain	Trinidad & Tobago	41
Port Said	Egypt	55
Port Sudan	Sudan	64
Port-au-Prince	Haiti	38
Port-de-Paix	Haiti	38
Port-Vila	Vanuatu	91
Portalegre	Portugal	27
Portland	United States	41
Pôrto Alegre	Brazil	44
Porto do Moniz	Madeira	59
Porto Novo	Benin	51
Porto Santo	Madeira	59
Porto-Alegre	São Tomé & Príncipe	63
Portobelo	Panama	39
Portoviejo	Ecuador	45
Portsmouth	United Kingdom	30
Portsmouth	Dominica	36
Poti	Georgia	72
Potnarhvin	Vanuatu	91
Potosí	Bolivia	44
Pottuvil	Sri Lanka	83
Poznan	Poland	26
Praia	Cape Verde	53
Praslin	St Lucia	40
Presov	Slovak Republic	27
Pretoria	South Africa	64
Prilep	Macedonia	25
Przhevalsk	Kyrgyzstan	77
Ptuj	Slovenia	28
Puebla	Mexico	39
Puerto Barrios	Guatemala	38
Puerto Cabezas	Nicaragua	39
Puerto Carreño	Colombia	45
Puerto Gortés	Honduras	38
Puerto la Cruz	Venezuela	47
Puerto Lempira	Honduras	38
Puerto Plata	Dominican Republic	37
Pujehun	Sierra Leone	63
Pula	Croatia	18
Punakha	Bhutan	71
Pune	India	74
Punta Arenas	Chile	45
Punta del Este	Uruguay	47
Punta Gorda	Belize	35
Puntarenas	Costa Rica	35
Pursat	Cambodia	72
Pusan	South Korea	76
Puttalam	Sri Lanka	83
Pyongyang	North Korea	76

Q

Qachas Nek	Lesotho	58
Qardho	Somalia	64
Qingdao	China	73
Qom	Iran	74
Qormi	Malta	25
Québec	Canada	36
Queenstown	New Zealand	89
Quelimane	Mozambique	61
Quetta	Pakistan	80
Quezaltenango	Guatemala	38
Quezon City	Philippines	81
Qui Nhon	Vietnam	85
Quito	Ecuador	45
Quthing	Lesotho	58

R

Rabat	Malta	25
Rabat	Morocco	61
Rabat(Gozo)	Malta	25
Rabaul	Papua New Guinea	90
Radom	Poland	26
Ramsgate	United Kingdom	30
Randers	Denmark	19
Rangoon	Myanmar	79
Ras ad Daqm	Oman	80
Ras al Khaimah	U.A.E.	85
Ras an Naqab	Jordan	76
Ras Laffan	Qatar	81
Rasht	Iran	74
Rawalpindi	Pakistan	80
Recife	Brazil	44
Redange	Luxembourg	24
Reggio di Calabria	Italy	23
Regina	Canada	36
Reno	United States	41
Reykjavík	Iceland	22
Rezekne	Latvia	24
Rhodes	Greece	22
Riaba	Equatorial Guinea	55
Riberalta	Bolivia	44
Richmond	United States	41
Riga	Latvia	24
Rijeka	Croatia	18
Rila	Bulgaria	18
Rincón	Costa Rica	35
Rio Branco	Brazil	44
Rio de Janeiro	Brazil	44
Riobamba	Ecuador	45
Rivera	Uruguay	47
Rivière du Rampart	Mauritius	60
Robertsport	Liberia	58
Roboré	Bolivia	44
Rocha	Uruguay	47
Rockhampton	Australia	88
Rome	Italy	23
Ronave	Nauru	89
Røros	Norway	26
Rosalie	Dominica	36
Rosario	Argentina	44
Rose Hill	Mauritius	60
Roseau	Dominica	36
Rosslare	Ireland	23
Rosso	Mauritania	60
Rostock	Germany	21
Rostov-on-Don	Russia	82
Rotterdam	Netherlands	26
Rovaniemi	Finland	21
Rovno	Ukraine	29
Roxborough	Trinidad & Tobago	41
Rubona	Rwanda	62
Ruhengeri	Rwanda	62
Ruse	Bulgaria	18
Rustavi	Georgia	72
Rutana	Burundi	52
Ruwais	Qatar	81
Ruwais	United Arab Emirates	85
Ruwayshid	Jordan	76
Ruyigi	Burundi	52
Rybnitsa	Moldova	25

S

Saarbrücken	Germany	21
Sabha	Libya	58
Sabiyah	Kuwait	77
Sad'ah	Yemen	85
Sadao	Thailand	84
Saint Joseph	Dominica	36
Saipan	Palau	90
Salalah	Oman	80
Salamanca	Spain	28
Salima	Malawi	59
Salisbury	Dominica	36
Salt	Jordan	76
Salt Lake City	United States	41
Salto	Uruguay	47
Salvador	Brazil	44
Salwah	Qatar	81
Salyany	Azerbaijan	70
Salzburg	Austria	16
Samara	Russia	82
Samarkand	Uzbekistan	85
Samsun	Turkey	29
San Antonio	Belize	35
San Antonio	United States	41
San Carlos de Bariloche	Argentina	44
San Cristóbal	Venezuela	47
San Diego	United States	41
San Fernando	Trinidad & Tobago	41
San Fernando de Apure	Venezuela	47
San Francisco	United States	41
San Fran. de Macorís	Dom. Republic	37
San Ignacio	Belize	35
San Jose	United States	41
San José	Costa Rica	35
San José	Guatemala	38
San José	Uruguay	47
San Juan	Dominican Republic	37
San Juan	Puerto Rico	40
San Marino	San Marino	23
San Miguel	El Salvador	37
San Pedro de Macorís	Dom. Rep.	37
San Pedro Sula	Honduras	38
San Salvador	El Salvador	37
San Vicente	El Salvador	37
Sana	Yemen	85
Sandakan	Malaysia	78
Sandy Point	St Christopher/Nevis	40
Sangre Grande	Trinidad & Tobago	41
Sanniquellie	Liberia	58
Sans-Souci	Haiti	38
Sant-Julià-de-Lòria	Andorra	16
Santa Ana	El Salvador	37
Santa Clara	Cuba	36
Santa Cruz	Bolivia	44
Santa Cruz	Azores	50
Santa Cruz	Canary Islands	52
Santa Cruz	Madeira	59
Santa Marta	Colombia	45
Santana	Madeira	59
Santander	Spain	28
Santarém	Portugal	27
Santarém	Brazil	44
Santiago	Dominican Republic	37
Santiago	Panama	39
Santiago	Chile	45
Santiago de Compostela	Spain	28
Santiago de Cuba	Cuba	36
Säntis	Switzerland	29
Santo Domingo	Dominican Rep.	37
São Luís	Brazil	44
São Paulo	Brazil	44
São Tomé	São Tomé and Príncipe	63
Sapporo	Japan	75
Sarajevo	Bosnia-Herzegovina	18
Sarandë	Albania	16
Sarh	Chad	53
Sarmiento	Argentina	44
Saskatoon	Canada	36
Sassandra	Côte D'Ivoire	54
Sauteurs	Grenada	38
Savalou	Benin	51
Savannakhet	Laos	78
Savé	Benin	51
Sayhut	Yemen	85
Scarborough	United Kingdom	30
Scarborough	Trinidad & Tobago	41
Schaan	Liechtenstein	24
Scoresbysund	Greenland	37
Seattle	United States	41
Sefadu	Sierra Leone	63
Ségou	Mali	60
Sekondi	Ghana	56
Selebi-Phikwe	Botswana	51
Seletar	Singapore	83
Semey	Kazakhstan	77
Sendai	Japan	75
Seoul	South Korea	76
Serangoon	Singapore	83
Seria	Brunei	72
Serravalle	San Marino	23
Serrekunda	Gambia	56
Setúbal	Portugal	27
Sevastopol	Ukraine	29
Seville	Spain	28
Sfax	Tunisia	66
Sha Tin	Hong Kong	73
Shanghai	China	73
Sharjah	United Arab Emirates	85
Sheffield	United Kingdom	30
Shek Wu Hui	Hong Kong	73
Shenyang	China	73
Shenzhen	China	73
Shibam	Yemen	85
Shiraz	Iran	74
Shkodër	Albania	16
Shuaiba	Kuwait	77
Shuwaikh	Kuwait	77
Siauliai	Lithuania	24
Sibenik	Croatia	18
Sibiti	Congo	54
Sidon	Lebanon	78
Siem Reap	Cambodia	72
Sigiriya	Sri Lanka	83
Siguiri	Guinea	57

City	Country	Page
Sikasso	Mali	60
Silgarhi	Nepal	80
Simferopol	Ukraine	29
Simla	India	74
Sines	Portugal	27
Singapore City	Singapore	83
Sinop	Turkey	29
Sinuiju	North Korea	76
Sisophon	Cambodia	72
Siteki	Swaziland	65
Sittwe	Myanmar	79
Sivas	Turkey	29
Siwa	Egypt	55
Skikda	Algeria	50
Skocjan	Slovenia	28
Skopje	Macedonia	25
Sligo	Ireland	23
Sodankyla	Finland	21
Sofia	Bulgaria	18
Sohar	Oman	80
Sokodé	Togo	65
Sokoto	Nigeria	62
Soldeu	Andorra	16
Solwezi	Zambia	67
Somerset	Bermuda	35
Søndre Strømfjord	Greenland	37
Songkhla	Thailand	84
Sonsonate	El Salvador	37
Sopron	Hungary	22
Soroki	Moldova	25
Soroti	Uganda	66
Souanké	Congo	54
Soufrière	St Lucia	40
Souillac	Mauritius	60
Sousse	Tunisia	66
Southampton	United Kingdom	30
Spanish Town	Jamaica	39
Speightstown	Barbados	34
Spitak	Armenia	70
Split	Croatia	18
Sri-Jayawardenapura	Sri Lanka	83
Srinagar	India	74
St Gallen	Switzerland	29
St George	Bermuda	35
St Georges	Grenada	38
St John's	Antigua & Barbuda	34
St John's	Canada	36
St Louis	United States	41
St Moritz	Switzerland	29
St Paul	United States	41
St Paul's	St Christopher/Nevis	40
St Paul's Bay	Malta	25
St. David's	United Kingdom	31
St. Louis	Senegal	63
St. Petersburg	Russia	82
Stanley	Hong Kong	73
Stara Zagora	Bulgaria	18
Stavanger	Norway	26
Stepanakert	Azerbaijan	70
Stip	Macedonia	25
Sto. António	São Tomé and Príncipe	63
Stockholm	Sweden	28
Strabane	United Kingdom	31
Stranraer	United Kingdom	31
Strasbourg	France	20
Strumica	Macedonia	25
Stung Treng	Cambodia	72
Stuttgart	Germany	21
Sucre	Bolivia	44
Suez	Egypt	55
Sukhumi	Georgia	72
Sukkur	Pakistan	80
Sumgait	Azerbaijan	70
Sundsvall	Sweden	28
Sunyani	Ghana	56
Sur	Oman	80
Surabaya	Indonesia	74
Surat Thani	Thailand	84
Suva	Fiji	88
Suzhou	China	73
Swakopmund	Namibia	61
Swansea	United Kingdom	31
Sydney	Australia	88
Szczecin	Poland	26
Szeged	Hungary	22
Székesfehérvár	Hungary	22

T

City	Country	Page
Ta'izz	Yemen	85
Tabeng	Cambodia	72
Tabernacle	St Christopher/Nevis	40
Tabora	Tanzania	65
Tabriz	Iran	74
Tachungnya	Northern Marianas	89
Tadjoura	Djibouti	54
Tadmur	Syria	83
Taegu	South Korea	76
Taejon	South Korea	76
Tahoua	Niger	62
Tai Po	Hong Kong	73
Taichung	Taiwan	84
Taif	Saudi Arabia	82
Tainan	Taiwan	84
Taipei	Taiwan	84
Taitung	Taiwan	84
Takamatsu	Japan	75
Takeo	Cambodia	72
Takoradi	Ghana	56
Talara	Peru	46
Talcahuano	Chile	45
Taldy-Kurgan	Kazakhstan	77
Tallinn	Estonia	20
Tamale	Ghana	56
Tamanrasset	Algeria	50
Tambacounda	Senegal	63
Tambora	Indonesia	74
Tampa	United States	41
Tampere	Finland	21
Tampico	Mexico	39
Tanapag	Northern Marianas	89
Tanga	Tanzania	65
Tangier	Morocco	61
Tanout	Niger	62
Taranto	Italy	23
Tarija	Bolivia	44
Tarim	Yemen	85
Tartu	Estonia	20
Tartus	Syria	83
Tashauz	Turkmenistan	84
Tashigang	Bhutan	71
Tashkent	Uzbekistan	85
Tbilisi	Georgia	72
Tegucigalpa	Honduras	38
Tehran	Iran	74
Tel Aviv	Israel	75
Telavi	Georgia	72
Tema	Ghana	56
Tenkodogo	Burkina Faso	51
Tete	Mozambique	61
Tétouan	Morocco	61
Tetovo	Macedonia	25
Teyateyaneng	Lesotho	58
Thakhek	Laos	78
The Crane	Barbados	34
The Hague	Netherlands	26
Thessaloniki	Greece	22
Thiès	Senegal	63
Thimphu	Bhutan	71
Thule	Greenland	37
Tianjin	China	73
Tibati	Cameroon	52
Tidjikdja	Mauritania	60
Tiemcen	Algeria	50
Tijuana	Mexico	39
Timaru	New Zealand	89
Timbuktu	Mali	60
Timisoara	Romania	27
Tindouf	Algeria	50
Tiranë	Albania	16
Tiraspol	Moldova	25
Toalanaro	Madagascar	59
Toamasina	Madagascar	59
Tobruk	Libya	58
Toco	Trinidad & Tobago	41
Tokyo	Japan	75
Toledo	Spain	28
Toliara	Madagascar	59
Tongsa	Bhutan	71
Tornio	Finland	21
Toronto	Canada	36
Tororo	Uganda	66
Tortosa	Spain	28
Torún	Poland	26
Toulouse	France	20
Tournai	Belgium	17
Tours	France	20
Townsville	Australia	88
Tozeur	Tunisia	66
Trabzon	Turkey	29
Tralee	Ireland	23
Travnik	Bosnia-Herzegovina	18
Trier	Germany	21
Triesen	Liechtenstein	24
Trieste	Italy	23
Trincomalee	Sri Lanka	83
Trinidad	Cuba	36
Trinidad	Bolivia	44
Tripoli	Libya	58
Tripoli	Lebanon	78
Tromsø	Norway	26
Trondheim	Norway	26
Trujillo	Honduras	38
Trujillo	Peru	46
Tsau	Botswana	51
Tsévié	Togo	65
Tshabong	Botswana	51
Tshane	Botswana	51
Tsuen Wan	Hong Kong	73
Tsumeb	Namibia	61
Tuas	Singapore	83
Tuasivi	Western Samoa	91
Tucker's Town	Bermuda	35
Tucumán	Argentina	44
Tuen Mun	Hong Kong	73
Tulcán	Ecuador	45
Tumaco	Colombia	45
Tumbes	Peru	46
Tunis	Tunisia	66
Turin	Italy	23
Turku	Finland	21
Turrialba	Costa Rica	35
Tutong	Brunei	72
Tuzla	Bosnia-Herzegovina	18
Tyre	Lebanon	78

U

City	Country	Page
Uaboe	Nauru	89
Ubon Ratchathani	Thailand	84
Udon Thani	Thailand	84
Uige	Angola	50
Ujung Pandang	Indonesia	74
Ulan Bator	Mongolia	79
Ullapool	United Kingdom	31
Umeå	Sweden	28
Umm al Qaiwain	U.A.E.	85
Umm Bab	Qatar	81
Umm Qasr	Kuwait	77
Umm Sai'd	Qatar	81
Uppsala	Sweden	28
Ura-Tyube	Tajikistan	84
Uralsk	Kazakhstan	77
Urumqi	China	73
Ushuaia	Argentina	44
Uskemen	Kazakhstan	77
Utrecht	Netherlands	26

V

City	Country	Page
Vaasa	Finland	21
Vacoas	Mauritius	60
Vaduz	Liechtenstein	24
Valdivia	Chile	45
Valencia	Spain	28
Valencia	Venezuela	47
Valladolid	Spain	28
Valletta	Malta	25
Valmiera	Latvia	24
Valparaíso	Chile	45
Vancouver	Canada	36
Vantaa	Finland	21
Varazdin	Croatia	18
Varna	Bulgaria	18
Vasteras	Sweden	28
Vatican City	Italy	23
Vatomandry	Madagascar	59
Växjö	Sweden	28
Veles	Macedonia	25
Venice	Italy	23
Ventspils	Latvia	24
Veracruz	Mexico	39
Viborg	Denmark	19
Victoria	Canada	36
Victoria	Grenada	38
Victoria	Seychelles	63
Vieng Sai	Laos	78
Vienna	Austria	16
Vientiane	Laos	78
Vieux Fort	St Lucia	40
Vigo	Spain	28
Vila do Porto	Azores	50
Villa Montes	Bolivia	44
Villarrica	Paraguay	46
Vilnius	Lithuania	24
Viña del mar	Chile	45
Vinh	Vietnam	85
Virovitica	Croatia	18
Vitebsk	Belarus	17
Vladivostok	Russia	82
Vlissingen	Netherlands	26
Vlorë	Albania	16
Vogan	Togo	65
Voi	Kenya	57
Voinjama	Liberia	58
Volgograd	Russia	82
Volos	Greece	22
Vorkuta	Russia	82
Vukovar	Croatia	18

W

City	Country	Page
Wad Medani	Sudan	64
Wadi Haifa	Sudan	64
Wajir	Kenya	57
Wallibu	St Vincent	40
Walvis Bay	Namibia	61
Wanganui	New Zealand	89
Warsaw	Poland	26
Washington	United States	41
Waterford	Ireland	23
Wau	Sudan	64
Wellington	New Zealand	89
Welshpool	United Kingdom	31
Wesley	Dominica	36
Weymouth	United Kingdom	30
Whangarei	New Zealand	89
Whitehorse	Canada	36
Wick	United Kingdom	31
Wiltz	Luxembourg	24
Windhoek	Namibia	61
Winnipeg	Canada	36
Winterthur	Switzerland	29
Wonsan	North Korea	76
Woodlands	Singapore	83
Worthing	Barbados	34
Wrexham	United Kingdom	31
Wroclaw	Poland	26
Wuhan	China	73

X

City	Country	Page
Xaafuun	Somalia	64
Xai-Xai	Mozambique	61
Xi'an	China	73
Xieng Khouang	Laos	78

Y

City	Country	Page
Yakutsk	Russia	82
Yamoussoukro	Côte D'Ivoire	54
Yangambi	Zaïre	66
Yangor	Nauru	89
Yaoundé	Cameroon	52
Yaren	Nauru	89
Yekaterinburg	Russia	82
Yellowknife	Canada	36
Yerevan	Armenia	70
Yeviakh	Azerbaijan	70
Yirga 'Alem	Ethiopia	55
Yogyakarta	Indonesia	74
Yokadouma	Cameroon	52
Yokohama	Japan	75
Yola	Nigeria	62
York	United Kingdom	30
Yuen Long	Hong Kong	73

Z

City	Country	Page
Zadar	Croatia	18
Zagreb	Croatia	18
Zahle	Lebanon	78
Zakataly	Azerbaijan	70
Zakopane	Poland	26
Zambezi	Zambia	67
Zamboanga	Philippines	81
Zanzibar	Tanzania	65
Zaporozhye	Ukraine	29
Zaragoza	Spain	28
Zarqa	Jordan	76
Zeebrugge	Belgium	17
Zémio	Central African Republic	53
Zenica	Bosnia-Herzegovina	18
Ziguinchor	Senegal	63
Zilina	Slovak Republic	27
Zinder	Niger	62
Zion	St Christopher/Nevis	40
Zomba	Malawi	59
Zouîrât	Mauritania	60
Zürich	Switzerland	29
Zvishavane	Zimbabwe	67
Zwedru	Liberia	58
Zwolle	Netherlands	26